FREE BOOKS

www.*forgottenbooks*.org

You can read literally thousands of books
for free at www.forgottenbooks.org

(please support us by visiting our web site)

Forgotten Books takes the uppermost care to preserve the entire content of the original book. However, this book has been generated from a scan of the original, and as such we cannot guarantee that it is free from errors or contains the full content of the original. But we try our best!

Truth may seem, but cannot be:
Beauty brag, but 'tis not she;
Truth and beauty buried be.

To this urn let those repair
That are either true or fair;
For these dead birds sigh a prayer.

Bacon

MASTERS OF MEDICINE

EDITED BY

ERNEST HART, D.C.L.

Masters of Medicine

Title.	Author.
JOHN HUNTER	*Stephen Paget*
WILLIAM HARVEY	*D'Arcy Power*
EDWARD JENNER	*Ernest Hart*
SIR JAMES SIMPSON	*H. Laing Gordon*
HERMANN VON HELMHOLTZ	*John G. McKendrick*
WILLIAM STOKES	*Sir William Stokes*
CLAUDE BERNARD	*Michael Foster*
SIR BENJAMIN BRODIE	*Timothy Holmes*
THOMAS SYDENHAM	*J. F. Payne*
VESALIUS	*C. Louis Taylor*

Masters of Medicine

JOHN HUNTER
MAN OF SCIENCE AND SURGEON

MASTERS OF
MEDICINE

JOHN HUNTER,

Man of Science and Surgeon

(1728—1793)

BY

STEPHEN PAGET

WITH INTRODUCTION
BY SIR JAMES PAGET

LONDON
T. FISHER UNWIN
PATERNOSTER SQUARE
MDCCCXCVII

EDWARDO BURD, M.D.

SALOPIENSI

CARISSIMÆ CONJUGIS PATRI

AMICO PATRIS CARISSIMI

DEDICO

PREFACE

MISS BAILLIE'S name must come first of those who have helped me. The Baillie manuscripts, her gift to the Royal College of Surgeons, are of the very highest value, full of facts about Hunter; and she has allowed me to publish other letters and papers concerning him from her private collection of autographs and records of her family.

Mr. J. B. Bailey, the late Librarian of the College, collected and gave to the Library a great number of photographs, drawings, newspaper cuttings, &c., relating to Hunter. I hope that I have made good use of them.

I thank Sir William MacCormac, President of the College, for permission to publish some of these letters and records; Mr. D'Arcy Power, who has most kindly looked over what I have written; Mr. Charles

PREFACE

Louis Taylor, assistant editor of this series, and Mr. Hewett, who have helped me in many ways. The praise of John Hunter, and the long list of his achievements, are known to all of us: I have only tried to draw a plain sketch of him as he was seen by the men of his own days.

London, *September*, 1897.

CONTENTS

		PAGE
	INTRODUCTION	13
I.	LONG CALDERWOOD, 1728–1748	19
II.	THE TWO BROTHERS	44
III.	LONDON, 1763–1771. GOLDEN SQUARE: EARL'S COURT	83
IV.	LONDON, 1772–1783. JERMYN STREET	95
V.	HUNTER AND JENNER	121
VI.	LONDON, 1783–1793. LEICESTER SQUARE	150
VII.	ST. GEORGE'S HOSPITAL	194
VIII.	AVE ATQUE VALE	220
IX.	AFTER HUNTER	235
	APPENDIX	261

(A) The Hunters and the Baillies.
(B) Chief References.

INTRODUCTION

IF we try to find, in Hunter's mental character, the facts to which may be ascribed his great influence in the promotion of medicine and surgery, I think it may justly be assigned to the degree in which he introduced the exercise of the observant scientific mind into the study and practice of surgery. In his own mind the chief attraction to science may be traced in his love of collecting. He collected "everything"—as it by natural disposition and in imitation of his brother William—but I think there is no evidence that he studied any part of his collection except that which became the Hunterian museum. This he studied in its widest range: and thus became—as no one else in his time was—a comparative anatomist and a pathologist; and he brought the knowledge of all that he thus acquired into union with his knowledge of medical and surgical practice. Through him, medicine and surgery came to be practically studied in the light of

INTRODUCTION

all these sciences. Naturally, he had been brought to the study of them after what may still be considered the best and most perfect system—that of scientific observation: he himself probably regarded it as only natural; but there is no clear evidence of his being self-studious.

Till he came to the teaching of other students, Hunter probably never taught himself any of the rules of scientific study: he was one of the few rare men to whom the love of carefully observing the course of Nature is sufficient for the motives and safe methods of scientific study.

For he saw the right method, and when he wanted to teach it he told it in words, quoted in Baron's Life of Jenner, "Don't think, try; be patient, be accurate;" plain words still useful in the whole range of medicine and of knowledge relating to it. We may believe that in what he read and what he heard in conversation with most of the leading medical men of his time, it was evident that they thought they could make what they believed to be knowledge more nearly complete, and more accurate, by "thinking" over what they already believed they knew to be true and fit to be expressed in "general principles." But the facts were rarely quite true; the general principles deduced from them were still more rarely true or safe for further guidance.

Hunter's rule may be well used in the promotion of all science. It so often seems safe to believe that by careful thinking over the facts already found and even

INTRODUCTION

repeatedly tested and confirmed, we may be able to think of others which appear naturally to follow them, and thus, by thinking, to enlarge our knowledge. But the history of science may teach that this is rarely safe ; and that every "thinking" must be "tried" patiently and carefully, by experiment or repeated careful observation, before it can be safely accepted as truth. Hunter held by this rule. He did indeed think ; he spent long times in only thinking ; but we may believe that in many of these long times his conclusion was that in thus thinking he was tempting himself to the wrong way, and that, at most, it could only suggest how he should patiently and carefully "try" what he had been led to think. Thus at least we may test his writings, and much of his museum work. The same may be held now ; facts are more numerous, and more nearly fully known ; but few are even now so complete as to be safe for generalising, and so it must yet be for a long time in all the divisions of medical science. The surety of every belief can only be sure after it has been "tried" by experiment or further observation.

The influence of Hunter may be observed in a comparison of the progress of medical science and practice in the present and in the last century. It is impossible to tell how much of the change may be due to him ; but the increase of accurate scientific observation, and the reliance on it rather than on theories, are clearly in accordance with his rule of study. And on the

INTRODUCTION

whole the amount of good done, as measurable at this time, has been greatest in proportion as it has been done by men working with scientific minds, both observing and thinking. Men have varied in their tendency to careful observation or to mere thinking; they have varied as have the several individual mental fitnesses or inclinations; but the general tendency has been to observation, to the accumulation of facts—as in the work of Pasteur and Lister.

This, then, was Hunter's chief distinction: that his mind was set on science, while his business was practical surgery. He was not, at first, scientific; he had mere business-teaching in his boyhood and a natural love of collecting; but, after maturity, he became scientific, and then was made constantly active in science by his continued love of collecting, and by the use of his collection for the advancement of pathology, and by the study of all structures even remotely connected with the specimens in his collection. Thus his mind, given to science, was engaged in practice; he associated surgery with science, and made them mutually illustrative. Before his time, surgeons had been "empirical"; and this word had been used not in its real sense of "experimental," but as meaning something discreditable, something not founded on "principles." Yet these "principles" were only thoughts exercised on insufficient facts, gradually but very slowly becoming more nearly sure, but hardly applicable from one century to the next.

INTRODUCTION

Each mind has its personal inclination—either toward thinking, or toward observation—and the one should be balanced by the other: that is, the complete scientific mind should be carefully observant, looking into everything, recording or collecting, and then thoughtfully repeating observations and comparing what had seemed most different; testing the observations in one range of facts by those in all others.

Therefore Hunter's lesson,—" Don't think, try,"—is admirable for all pursuit of science; a great contribution to scientific work, from one who was a surgeon, and most truly a "naturalist." For, in all retrospects of medical practice, where one sees the continued use of modes of treatment now deemed useless or mischievous—such as long or frequent bleeding, either local or general—there was no want of *thinking* that these were useful. So with the frequent use of mercury and of purgatives, there were ample "reasons" for these methods of practice; and the reasons seemed so good that observations were really not made. The thinking was clearer than the facts; the thinking determined the observations, till the facts became too frequent and too hard; and *then*, commonly, the real facts were for a time put aside.

JAMES PAGET.

JOHN HUNTER

I

Long Calderwood. 1728–1748.

"I believe that I was in many ways a naughty boy. . . . The school as a means of education to me was simply a blank."—DARWIN.

WE who write this series of the "Masters of Medicine" must address all readers, and set forth the work of the Masters as physicians and surgeons; but we cannot offer to everybody an unreserved account of the processes of disease and their treatment. I will do my best, avoiding this offence, to steer clear of the opposite folly of giving a trivial or gossiping account of John Hunter.

He came of a very old Scotch family, probably of Norman origin, the Hunters of Hunterston in Ayrshire, whose history goes back to the thirteenth century. The old manor-house of Hunterston, with its tower of great antiquity, is still standing; once a stronghold, now a farm-house. The Hunters of Long Calderwood in Lanarkshire were a younger branch of this family, through Francis Hunter, grandfather of John Hunter. Long Calderwood is a small estate, seven miles from Glasgow, and one mile north of the village of East Kilbride; with a good stone house, two stories high. Here John Hunter, son of John Hunter, was born on February 13, 1728,[1] the last of ten children. Death came again and again to Long Calderwood: of all the brothers and sisters—John, Elizabeth, Andrew, Janet, James, Agnes, William, Dorothea, Isabella, and John—the first three died in childhood, and four others—Janet, James, Agnes, and Isabella—died in the prime of life.

Of their father, Dr. Matthew Baillie said that he was a man of good understanding, of great integrity, and of an anxious temper. There is a portrait of him in the entrance hall of the Royal College of Surgeons, which was originally drawn in crayons by his son James, and was afterward copied in oils for his son William. Their mother, Agnes, was a daughter of Mr. Paul, a maltster, and treasurer of the City of Glasgow: "a woman of great worth and of considerable talents." (M. Baillie.)

[1] The parish register says the 13th; he himself observed the 14th as his birthday, and that is the day of the Hunterian Oration at the Royal College of Surgeons. Probably he was born during the night of the 13th–14th, and in the room over the kitchen. A report of the house, written in 1867, says that it has not changed since 1728, except that it was then thatched and is now slated, and two rooms downstairs have been thrown into one.

LONG CALDERWOOD, 1728-1748

The home at Long Calderwood could afford only what was most necessary for the children :—

"Their father, from the expenses of a large family, altho' managed with great frugality, was occasionally obliged to sell portions of his estate. This increased the constitutional anxiety of his mind, and he was often kept awake in the night from thinking upon the difficulties of his situation."

James, the first son who lived to grow up, died of phthisis when he was twenty-nine years old. He was handsome, clever, and beloved by all of them; and William Hunter used to say that he was the cleverest of the family, and that if he had lived nothing could have prevented him from being the first physician in London. He was educated to be a Writer to the Signet; but he gave up law for medicine, and went to London, and began to work at anatomy, living with William; then broke down with hæmorrhage from the lungs, went home in 1743, and died there.

Janet married a young timber merchant, named Buchanan, who had come from London and settled in business at Glasgow. He was good-looking, unbusinesslike, and fond of society; and there is a further charge against him, that he "joined to his other companionable talents the unfortunate endowment of a good voice and a musical ear." Having become bankrupt, he took to teaching music in Glasgow; "and besides teaching, was appointed Clerk to an Episcopalian Society of Christians. To this day he is recollected by the familiar name of *Amen.*" (Adams.) Janet died within a year after her marriage, and left no child; and Buchanan, in his old age, married again.

Dorothea was more happy in her husband; she married the Rev. James Baillie, the minister at Hamilton, near Kilbride, afterward Doctor of Divinity and Professor of Divinity (November, 1775) at Glasgow. He died in 1778, leaving his wife poor. They had three children, Matthew, Agnes, and Joanna. Matthew became a famous physician in London, a "Master of Medicine" whose name is still honoured. Joanna had the gift of poetry, and was of great renown in her day; she was "the immortal Joanna," one of Sir Walter Scott's closest friends. Agnes lived to the extreme old age of a hundred years and seven months.

William was of himself enough to make the name of Hunter for ever memorable. He too was one of the Masters of Medicine. If John did at last surpass him, it was William who set him on the way to do it: and until John Hunter went to London, William was the Elder Brother of the parable, and John was the 'Prodigal Son, in the Kingdom of Science.[1]

[1] And in the little home-kingdom of Long Calderwood there was, we may believe, the same difference between them. See the reminiscences of their niece, Mrs. Joanna Baillie, at the end of this chapter. Note that those children who lived to grow up had pet names—James was Jamie, Dorothea was Dolly, Agnes was Nannie, Isabella was Tibbie, John was Jockie or Johnny at Long Calderwood and Jack in London, William was Willie.

LONG CALDERWOOD, 1728–1748

William was born ten years before John, on May 23, 1718. He was diligent at school; and in 1731 went with a bursary to Glasgow College for five years. Then he began to read for the ministry, but changed his mind, and made application to be schoolmaster in his native village, and happily failed to get the appointment. Next came his friendship with Cullen, in the days when Cullen had yet to make a name; and from 1737 to 1740 William lived with him at Hamilton, helping him in the uphill work of a scattered country practice.[1] "His conversation was remarkably lively and agreeable, and his whole conduct was more strictly and steadily correct than that of any other young person I have ever known:" this was Cullen's estimate of him. In 1740, he attended Alexander Monro's lectures at Edinburgh; in the summer of 1741, he set his face toward London. Here he lived for a short time with Dr. Smellie, of Lanark, who had come to London two years before him, and was laying the foundations of great success, practising as an apothecary and accoucheur, having a shop in Pall Mall. Then he became assistant to Dr. John Douglas, and was resident in his house on the Piazza, Covent Garden; and entered as a surgeon's pupil at St. George's

[1] "Their principal ambition was to procure the means of improving their medical education and grade; and in order to further this honourable object it was stipulated that one of them should be allowed to study during the winter in some medical school, while the other should continue to carry on the business in the country, for the profit of both parties." ("Lives of British Physicians," London, John Murray, 1830.)

Hospital, which was then only seven years old, and as a dissecting pupil under Dr. Frank Nicholls: he also attended lectures on experimental philosophy. Next year, 1742, Dr. Douglas died. William Hunter still lived with the family, and was paying his addresses to Miss Douglas, and acting as tutor and guardian of her brother. In 1743, he contributed his first paper to the Transactions of the Royal Society, "On the Structure and Diseases of Articulating Cartilages."

There was at this time a society of naval surgeons in London, who met at a house in Covent Garden to hear Samuel Sharpe lecture on the operations of surgery. He gave up the lectures, from ill-health, and increase of practice; and in 1746 William Hunter took his place, and added to the course on operative surgery a set of lectures on anatomy. Here is the advertisement of them, from the London *Evening Post*, of January 9–12, 1748:—

> On Monday, the 1st of February, at Five in the Afternoon,
> Will Begin
> A COURSE OF ANATOMICAL LECTURES,
> To which will be added, the Operations of Surgery, with the Application of Bandages.
> By WILLIAM HUNTER, Surgeon.
> Gentlemen may have an Opportunity of learning the Art of Dissecting during the whole Winter Season, in the same manner as at Paris.

LONG CALDERWOOD, 1728–1748

Printed Proposals to be delivered at Mr. Millar's, Bookseller, opposite to the End of Katherine Street in the Strand.

He made about seventy guineas in fees for his first course : a larger sum of money, he said, than he had ever been master of before ; but the money went to help his friends, and in 1747 he had to put off the lectures for a fortnight, because he could not afford to pay for the advertisement of them. That year (August 6) he was admitted to the Corporation or Surgeons of London : and in 1748[1] made a tour through Holland to Paris, and on his way visited Albinus at Leyden. He came back to London in time to prepare his lectures for the winter ; and in September, a fortnight before the course began, John Hunter joined him.

Their father did not live to see the beginning of their success; he died on December 30, 1741, seventy-eight years old. Their mother died on November 3, 1751, aged sixty-six. At the Royal College of Surgeons there is a letter from the father, only three months before his death, to William Hunter : on the question whether he should come home and enter into partnership with Cullen, or stop in London and be assistant to Dr. Douglas. The letter is in James's handwriting, only signed by the father :—

"Nothing has proved a greater comfort than the

[1] This is the date assigned to the tour by Simmons, on good evidence. William also went to Paris with young John Douglas, soon after Dr. Douglas's death in 1742. See the letters at the end of this chapter.

hopes of seeing you here soon; but your letter has cast a very great damp upon us all. . . . I surely must soon expect to be beyond this side of time, considering my age and present indisposition, being for some days past confined to my bed with sickness, and a severe fit of the gravel, and would be glad to have you near me for the little while I shall be in this world; though at the same time I should be sorry to hinder you from making your way in the world, the best way you can. I wish you to consider well what you do. With Dr. Cullen you may be very comfortably settled, and make money, and if you miss this opportunity now, you cannot be sure of it at another time. Dr. Douglas's kind offer is only for a time. He may die before you come home or are settled, and leave you without friends at a great enough uncertainty. I suppose now you know very well the difference between the expense of living at home and abroad, and that perhaps cloaths and pocket-money may cost you more than your whole expense at home would do. You know my willingness to assist you, but you know too, that already I have gone fully as far as my numerous family will allow of. You must now do something for yourself. Consider all these things, and if you can persuade me that it is for your good, I will not be against it."

The old home at Long Calderwood passed through many hands after the father's death: it came to James, to William, to Matthew Baillie, to John, to his son, and to Matthew Baillie's son, William Hunter Baillie;

LONG CALDERWOOD, 1728–1748

to whose daughter, Miss Baillie, it now belongs. It was Mrs. Joanna Baillie's home for a time; and it was John Hunter's world till he was seventeen years old.

Throughout his boyhood he was good at such games as the village afforded to boys, and observant of Nature; but deficient in self-control, idle, and ignorant—a great disgrace for a Scots boy living within walking distance of Glasgow College, whose father was a gentleman, whose brothers were studying law and medicine. He afterward said of himself: "When I was a boy, I wanted to know all about the clouds and the grasses, and why the leaves changed colour in the autumn; I watched the ants, bees, birds, tadpoles, and caddis-worms; I pestered people with questions about what nobody knew or cared anything about." He hated his school-books; nor did he see the good of learning even at Oxford, in a couple of months that he wasted there long after boyhood was over. "They wanted to make an old woman of me, or that I should stuff Latin and Greek at the University; but these schemes I cracked like so many vermin as they came before me."

When he was seventeen, he went for a short time to the Buchanans at Glasgow, and amused himself in the timber-yard, but did not set his hand to anything, and soon returned home. At last, when he was getting on for twenty, he came to himself, and London began calling in his ears, as is her way with all the best men in Scotland. He wrote to William, asking leave to come and work under him; else he would enlist in the Army. He got a kindly answer, bidding him come and stay. He started at once, riding with Francis Hamilton, a friend of the family; and in September, 1748, the two brothers joined hands to work together in London.

I.

From a Letter written by Mrs. Joanna Baillie.

... Dr. William Hunter was the son of John Hunter of Long Calderwood in the parish of Kilbride, this place being a small possession upon which he lived many years, and the only remaining one, of several which he had purchased in or near the same parish, that he died possessed of.

I mention this, because it has been said by mistake in one of the late published lives of John Hunter, that this small farm or estate had been in the possession of the family for several generations; whereas Dr. Hunter's Father, who was the son of a younger son of the family of Hunterston obliged from some domestic unhappiness to leave his home at an early age, had no patrimony of any kind, and the money which enabled the Doctor's Father to purchase lands—which the pressure of a large family that he wished to educate liberally obliged him afterwards to sell—arose from *his* Father marrying a woman who was in those days a pretty considerable heiress.

LONG CALDERWOOD, 1728-1748

William Hunter, whilst a boy and a young man in his Father's house, was of a diligent and careful disposition, indefatigable in making himself master of anything that he wished to know, but at the same time having a great relish for everything droll or characteristic, and taking great pleasure in conversing with the country people in the neighbourhood, and amusing himself with their peculiarities, which he had a particular turn for drawing out. He was of principles to be depended upon at all times for doing what is right, affectionate to his family, and ready to lift up his hand in defence of his brothers and sisters, but not of that frank and open disposition which makes those of less steady principles and weaker affections more beloved.

His elder brother, James Hunter, who died in the twenty-ninth year of his age, a man of the most promising abilities, handsome in his person, and so engaging in his manners that his friends—amongst whom were Dr. Smollett and Dr. Cullen—always spoke of him with strong marks of attachment and admiration, being looked upon by his Father as the son most likely to make his way in the world was sent to Edinburgh to be bred to the Law, and intended for a Writer; whilst William was destined for a quieter profession requiring a less expensive education, and became a student of divinity for the Scotch Kirk. This, however, he quitted after some time, and from motives of conscience, we have good reason to believe, rather than from fickleness. Having a disposition to examine thoroughly every subject he wished to be connected with, he read a great deal of theology and Church controversy, and, in consequence of it, imbibed the opinions of Arius, which were probably strengthened by the conversations of a brother of his Mother's, a man of some learning, and strongly attached to those opinions.

I have asked my Mother whether she remembers any anecdotes of his youth that could throw light upon his character, but if there are any that might have been remembered, they have now escaped from her, and cannot be recovered. In regard to one circumstance her memory is not at all impaired, that he was to her a steady friend and affectionate brother, and to her children a steady and liberal benefactor. She adds that to her certain knowledge, though putting a considerable value upon money, and having always before him some object for which he wished to spend it, he not unfrequently accommodated his friends with considerable sums, and at one time when he had been rather blamed as not being grateful to the Widow of a Friend to whom he lay under great obligations, it was found after the Lady's death, upon examining her papers, that the accusation was unjust.

John Hunter was nearly ten years younger than his brother William, and the youngest of a large Family. Being the youngest, and a very great favourite of his Mother, whilst his Father—who was an old man and suffering very much from disease for some years before his death—could attend to him but little, he was extremely indulged, and so humoursome that he would often, when a pretty big boy, sit for hours together crying when he could not get what he wanted; and could not be taught to read but with the greatest difficulty, and long after the age when other children read English fluently, and have even made some progress in Latin. However, great as his aversion was to his book, he was by no means considered as a stupid boy; and tho' retaining, long past the age when such things are tolerated, that childish habit of crying, when occasion called upon him he was bold and intrepid, which the following little anecdote will show.

One night, when he was about twelve years old, having gone to chat a little with some neighbours who lived in a cottage near his Father's house, whilst he was sitting by the fire with two or three country people, a most terrible apparition, with a face resembling the Devil's, opened the door and looked in upon them. The company, which consisted of a woman and two men, believing it really to be what it represented, were petrified with fear and remained immoveable; but John Hunter—who was, as he confessed afterwards, by no means certain that it was not the Devil—snatched the tongs from the hearth, and attacking the spectre, made it roar with pain and run out of the house. This terrible figure proved to be a man dressed up with a painted mask, which in those days none of the country people would have any idea of ; and so terrible was the face, that amongst the people which he visited that night, going about from one cottage to another, one man fevered immediately, and died of the fright.

Before his Father's death, he was sent to a Latin school at Kilbride, where his Brothers had been taught with success, but making no progress at all, he was taken away from it. After his Father's death he remained an idle, uneducated Boy upon his Mother's hands, who—though a sensible woman and one who had been herself much better educated than women generally were in those days, being taught Music and other accomplishments not so common then as they are now—had, from her great indulgence, but little influence over him, notwithstanding he was by no means destitute of warm affections.

Her husband, eldest son, and greater part of the family being now dead, her second son William gone to push his way in London, and the property of the family much reduced by the expenses of education and sickness, &c., she had now to consider what she should do with a lad who showed great neatness of hands and quickness of perception in anything that regarded mechanism, but remained obstinately impenetrable to everything in the form of book-learning. She therefore, with the advice of her friends, sent him to Glasgow, to be some time with a relation, with whom he continued for a short time.

LONG CALDERWOOD, 1728–1748

II.

From a Letter written by Mrs. Agnes Baillie to her brother, Dr. Matthew Baillie.

My Mother's family came from an old Family of that name, in Ayrshire, Hunter of Hunterstone; the Laird from which our immediate Ancestor sprung had been 3 times married and had a Family by all his Wives; our immediate branch came from a second son of the first marriage, so that except the eldest son, who by entail inherited the landed property, all the rest were obliged to shift for themselves.

My mother's mother was the daughter of Mr. Paul, one of the Baillies of the City of Glasgow; he was also the Treasurer, and had the superintendence of all the Public Works carried on by the City during his being in Office.

Your uncle William went to try his fortune in London, with good recommendations; and Dr. Douglas, who was one of the first medical practitioners in London, took him into his family, as an Assistant in his dissection-room and in the surgery. Here he made himself so useful from his skill, and fine hands in operating, and ingratiated himself so much with the family, that Dr. Douglas did not object to his paying his addresses to his daughter Miss Douglas —which marriage never took place, as she died soon after it was agreed upon.[1] Dr. Douglas's son, who it

[1] "Mrs. Douglas survived her husband till May 5, 1752. Her daughter,

would appear was intended for the Medical line, was sent over to Paris for his improvement, for then the French were the best anatomists, from their greater facility in procuring Bodies to dissect, and from their instruments being better—as then they far excelled us in Cutlery, as much as we do them now in both. Young Douglas was very dissipated and would do nothing, so after being in France for some time they returned.

Your uncle, at his return, set up for himself: his first house was in Covent Garden, his dissection-room behind. Here he very soon was known as the best Anatomist and Accoucheur in London—to the great dislike of the English Surgeons, who could not bear that two Scotch-men should presume to rival them: for another Scotchman, a Dr. Smellie from Lanerk, had settled in London in Wardour-street a few years before, and succeeded very well. Dr. Hunter was the second, and he did still better; but when his brother John came up—and by his excellent hands and head for dissection—the anger of the English practitioners knew no bounds, and learning that he had been with a Brother-in-Law who was a Carpenter (altho' that was quite untrue) they said he was an ignorant Carpenter—however, that did not hinder him from becoming the first Anatomist of this or any age.

Martha Jane Douglas, died in 1744, aged 28; her son, James Douglas, ruined himself by his indiscretion, and died about the year 1755, aged 30 years." (Simmons.)

LONG CALDERWOOD, 1728-1748

Your uncle William was the first man that ever attended any Queen in the Country—Queen Charlotte had been attended by a Woman in her first confinement—and these Medical Ladies were well educated for their profession, and were commonly the Daughters of Medical Men or Clergymen's Daughters.

John Hunter was the youngest son, and his Mother spoiled him. He would do nothing but what he liked, and neither liked to be taught reading nor writing nor any kind of learning, but rambling amongst the woods, braes, &c., looking after Birds'-nests, comparing their eggs—number, size, marks, and other peculiarities : whilst his two elder brothers had both been to College, and got the same education that the sons of country gentlemen then got.

My Mother's eldest sister Janet was very handsome, and after refusing one of the best matches in Glasgow married Mr. Buchanan, a young handsome Man, with a very good Patrimony, and a branch of an old Family of that name. He had, along with others as partners, a large wood or timber-yard—where seasoned Wood ready for building Houses could always be had, and also, which was the custom of the times, wood of all kinds for making Furniture, Mahogany, Walnut, and other sorts, properly seasoned for making the Furniture : for in those days there was no such thing as an Upholsterer. So in the Wood-yard there were Carpenters, of all sorts, for making Tables, Chests of Drawers, Book-cases, according to the taste of their

JOHN HUNTER

Customers : and those old antique Wardrobes, with heavy carved work, now valued as Antiques, were the workmanship of these branches of the trade.

At his sister's marriage, Johnny, as they called him, being quite unsettled, was sent down to his sister's, to see what could be made of him. So it was natural, as he was very curious and ingenious, when it pleased him, to go frequently into the workshop, amongst the carpenters there, and try his hand, and I daresay he did : but no scrap of paper, or letter, or anything my Mother ever said, gave the least intimation of anything as to his being bred to it. At any rate, he had but a very short time of it—for he went to stay with his sister after the marriage, and she died before the twelvemonth was over—and he returned before her death—so that he was but a very few months with his Brother-in-law, Mr. Buchanan—and was only about seventeen when he went to his brother Dr. William Hunter in London. . . . As for Mr. Buchanan, as he spent his fortune in giving dinners, and in going to them—where his very fine voice was an attraction the gentlemen of Glasgow were not accustomed to—his fortune was spent, he became insolvent, and after leading a very various life, sometimes a Precentor in Church singing and giving out the Psalms, and sometimes another occupation, he when an old man married a Lady of good family and with a pretty good Fortune.

LONG CALDERWOOD, 1728-1748

III.

From William Hunter to his Mother.

DR. MOTHER,—Jamie and I have both great comfort from your letters, and we hope you'l continue to write often yourself and influence our sisters to follow your example. Jamie approves of your conduct very much, and returns you the inclosed which he has subscribed. If I could have thought that Dr. Douglas' death would have come to your ears so soon, I should have prevented the fears you may have had on this occasion. 'Tis in vain to say that neither Jamie or I are losers by the accident ; but still we are in a very good way. Jamie is just falling upon a way of supporting himself here in London honestly and genteely ; and at last I'm perswaded will be able to do something honourable to himself and reputable to his relations. Those who have been his friends in Scotland will 'tis hoped in a few years rejoice with him, and if he had any ennimys 'tis to be fear'd that their own hands and a halter will become their onely surviving well-wishers.

You'l no doubt wish to hear of my affairs, and to satisfy you I'll be a little particular. Tho' Dr. Douglas during his short sickness minded his worldly concerns but little, yet he died not without recommending me warmly to his family. No friends or relations were admitted to see him, his fever being tumultuous and precipitant, and leaving him onely a few intervals of ease or tolerable composure of mind. During the last of these I received orders from him of being in the way, and that he wanted to speak with me as soon as his head was a little settled. But immediately I had another message telling me he was worse and must defer seeing me. This was the night before his death. Early next morning I was call'd at his desire, when he thought himself pretty easy. I went in, he snatch'd my hand, and spoke a few words with too great affection for his giddy disorder. Immediately his fancy wander'd, and tho' he could not talk sensibly, yet he still knew me, and would not let me go out of the room. I sat on his bed till after noon, when he expir'd with his hand locked in mine. At his death I had mournings and a Ring from Mrs. Douglas. Then I was told that on his death-bed he acquainted the family that I should go to Paris, and that I must go. At present I sleep and eat with the young Dr., his son, and in Harvest I go to France with him, if a war does not prevent our intension for one season. I have the happiness of being aggreable to the whole family so far as I can guess by their beheaveour. After I come from Paris I have a scheme laid out of settling here, and certainly nobody can say that it will not succeed. But I'll say no more of projects lest you think me a Castle builder.

I'm heartily concerned for my little dear sister Tibbie, but I hope the Mare's milk and the Fole together will surely recover her, for you know she likes Foles and Calfs. Tell her she must write me about the White Hamilton Stork, and that Jamie and I will pay her a visit as soon as we have got our pockets full of gold to buy her a country seat, and give her what horses or other things she wants. My Brother and I remember you all with great love. I am

>Dear Mother
>>Your Affectionate Son
>>>WILLIAM HUNTER.

LONDON, *June 3d* 1742.

IV.

From William Hunter to James Hunter.

Addressed, To Mr James Hunter, Longcalderwood, To the care of the Post Master of Hamilton, North Britain.

DEAR JAMIE,—'Tis now after dinner, I have a great deal to do, and we take Coach tomorrow by 4 in the morning, so you have as little reason to expect a connected Letter, as a short one. . . . I have not time for endeavouring to be humorous, tho' I know you have a great Gusto that way; but faith that is what I make as little progress in as drawing; I like both and think both easy, but when I attempt either I throw aside my pen or pencill, and snuff as voraciously as James Warnok's Wife would swallow meal, seed and all, out of another person's pock at the

Mill. But to dispatch, I have just received a Letter from dear Dr. Cullen which gives me a deal of concern, and indeed so much that I wish it had miscarried. I heartily pity him, and wish him all happiness, and am sorry I can neither help nor well advise him ; but pray comfort him. As to yourself, I beg again and again that you will persecute your studies with resolution and never fear the event. I cannot learn why you throw Monro out of your scheme. I really think his a good course, and so fit for you that I would by no means have you neglect it, except you cannot otherwise attend enough to Pharmacy and Surgery which are truly the chief points. As to all my friends in Scotland especially in Longcalderwood and Glasgow, let them know I pray for them and that they ought to pray too for me, and my prosperity in the world ; because I shall always think it the happiness of Riches to support Relations ; not only to assist them, but make them sharers in the greatest prosperity. May God for their sakes second my endeavours ! But to leave off writing, tho' I shall never cease thinking of my dear Mother Sisters and Brothers, let me now tell you something of my own affairs. . . . I have taken leave of all the great men with a deal of satisfaction, and indeed I have the pleasure of thinking that every soul of my acquaintance wish me well and would be ready to serve me, at least I have of late had many protestations and some examples of this kind. My dear Jamie you who

LONG CALDERWOOD, 1728-1748

know that my duty is to communicate all to you will excuse my freedom and attribute nothing of this to vanity. The kindness that I have met with in this family of late is infinitely more than I deserve and a great deal more than I expected. In your prayers put in a word for good Mrs. Douglas. I need not mention particulars but everything will be to my wish. But as I have now given you my past History I must now let you into my views after I come home. I need not tell you that John Douglas died about 2 months agoe, and communicated his knowledge in the cure of venereal disorders to Dr. Owen, who managed all his business in that way during his Illness and has carried it on since his Death for the Widow's benefit. This gentleman you know married Dr. Douglas' Dau^r. As he was not capable for the surgery part, and wanted to be in the country during the summer seasons, he choosed to have a partner. The offer was made me, and after consulting Dr. Armstrong, Mr. Smellie, and my own inclinations, I accepted of it. . . . I thought it the only way to settle in my darling London, to give Lectures and be useful to you or Jockie. . . . The proposals are that we keep John Douglas' house, which Dr. Owen is to go into this winter, and I am to succeed him in the Spring when he goes out of Town. The house is to be fitted up with Dr. Owen's own furnishing, so that I shall be at no expenses on that score, and he is to have a footman at his own expense likewise. The house-rent, Taxes, and maid-keeping, which will come to £60 per An., is to be a common burthen, as are Medicines, &c. On the other hand all the profits are to be equally divided, and if the profits of the first year do not discharge the expenses I am neither to receive nor pay ; so that upon the whole I think I am upon a very good footing. I have no more time and therefore can neither tell you what friends desire to be remembered to you nor what Blessings I send to you all. Once more let me pray for all happiness to the dear family, and then Farewell.

WILLIAM HUNTER.

LONDON, *Sept.* 17*th.*

In London, June 22, 1744, William wrote again to James, giving a long account of the journey to Paris, *viâ* Calais, Boulogne, Montreuil, Abbeville, and Amiens ; with a description of Chantilly, the vineyards, and much beside. "I'm heartily glad to hear that you are in the recruiting way. I wish you all pleasures in your Whey-drinking ; and indeed, from the accounts I have had of these expeditions, I'm perswaded you will pass time very agreeably. There you will be introduced to my dear Idol *Nature,* simplex munditiis. There you can with more attention observe the handywork of that Lady's fond father. Every Rock will seem his strong tower, every flower his little fairy mistress. Believe me I could wish to accompany you. . . ."

LONG CALDERWOOD, 1728–1748

These is also, in the College of Surgeons, a letter from James to William (March 24, 1741) giving an account of the death of their sister Nannie (Agnes). She died on Sunday, March 20th.

. . . If you happen to see any print or picture resembling her in London, I beg you'll mind to purchase it. . . . As Nannie was averse to my going into the Army, at any rate I'll delay it for some time upon her account ; and as she was always fond of my engaging with the painting, I'll humour her and try it. I expect you won't neglect every opportunity of writing, they give incredible pleasure to the whole family, and I am sure you would not willingly let slip any occasion of comforting them at this time. Take care of your health, my dear Willie, forget not to pray to Nannie, imagine you have a Sister in Heaven who is as able I hope as willing to hear and do for her friends here. Farewell.

    I am
        Your dear brother
            JAMES HUNTER.

II

THE TWO BROTHERS.

"Who then are the men in the profession, that would persuade students that a little of Anatomy is enough for a physician, and a little more, too much for a surgeon? God help them! They have it not themselves, and are afraid that others should get it."—WILLIAM HUNTER.

THOUGH the two Hunters were far apart in temperament, yet we seem always to see them together; we know they went different ways at the last, but we feel that they followed the same star, up to the day when William Hunter, on his death-bed, had his brother back again at his side, and said, "If I had strength enough to hold a pen, I would write how easy and pleasant a thing it is to die." This chapter is therefore given to some account of their work together, and the later years of the elder brother's life.

That they were not of the same temperament is shown by their portraits. Reynolds, Zoffany,[1] and Pine have presented William Hunter as a fine

[1] William Hunter is the chief figure in Zoffany's picture of the Academicians round the model in the Life-school; which was exhibited in 1772. The portrait of him, attributed to Zoffany, in the Royal College of Surgeons, is a replica of the Reynolds portrait at Glasgow.

THE TWO BROTHERS

gentleman, well dressed, carefully posed. His hands are delicate, his features are regular and remarkably handsome: in the portrait by Reynolds, his mouth has become thin and very sensitive, his eyes have an air of fatigue, his whole look is sharpened and restless. These pictures are in notable contrast with Robert Home's portrait of John Hunter. Home has painted him in his working dress, a loose dissecting-apron with long sleeves; the cuffs are turned back, the garment is caught round him anyhow with a single button; his attitude is clumsy, and he seems to be in a hurry to be gone; his features have none of his brother's good looks, they want fineness; but the whole face and figure are full of indomitable strength.

The brothers began work together in September, 1748: about which time William Hunter wrote to Cullen—"I want to tell you many things about colleges, hospitals, professorships, chariots, wives, &c., &c. I'm busy in forming a plan for being an author. In short, my head is full of a thousand things." The winter course was to begin in a fortnight: William set his brother to show his skill at dissection, was delighted with it, and made him assistant in the dissecting-rooms. That same year William Hunter was appointed physician-accoucheur to the Middlesex Hospital, and, next year, surgeon-accoucheur to the British Lying-in Hospital. Fortune was prepared to favour him, and after her usual fashion, at the expense of others, his seniors in the practice of midwifery. Dr. Smellie had the advantage of him in experience, had been lecturing and writing these many years; but "his person is said to have been coarse, and his manners awkward and unpleasing"; and Fortune had treated William Hunter more generously. Sir Richard Manningham was growing old, and died in 1759 : Dr. Sandys, about the same time, retired from practice. The furious opposition of the midwives to men practising midwifery was coming to an end. All was going well with him : in 1750 he graduated Doctor of Physic at his old University ; in 1751 he was admitted to the Faculty of Physicians and Surgeons of Glasgow ; and that summer he went home to Long Calderwood, now by the death of James his own property, saw his mother—she died in November of this year—and visited Cullen ; then came back to London, bade farewell to the Douglases, and settled in practice at 42, Jermyn Street.

John Hunter, in these three busy years, 1748—1751, was laying the foundations of his power over anatomy, and for his lighter studies was seeing something of the hospital practice of Cheselden and Pott. Already William Hunter had made a man of him, but not yet a gentleman [1] : John had given himself body and

[1] "He was fond of company, and mixed much in the society of young men of his own standing, and joined in that sort of dissipation which men at his age, and freed from restraint, are but too apt to indulge in. Nor was he always very nice in the choice of his associates, but sometimes sought entertainment in the coarse, broad humour to be found

mind to his task in the dissecting-rooms : " he did not work in Anatomy, as is usually done, for a few hours in the day, but was employed in it from the rising to the setting of the sun." When the winter course of 1749 began, he was advanced to be demonstrator to the students : thus, only a year after he left home, he held in his hands the honour of the new school. It was but a few years old, a private venture, unendowed, unsupported by any hospital ; but the two young men together drove it on to success : and the younger brother bore the rough work, hobnobbing with the resurrection-men, slaving all day long in unwholesome air, dissecting, demonstrating, and putting up specimens. This giving of demonstrations is an arduous office, and in Hunter's time it was horribly unwholesome. For example, Jesse Foot wrote in 1794 : "Within these last ten years, five lecturers in Anatomy are now fresh upon my memory, who have fallen the victims of putrid *myasma* in the prime of life."

But the end of the winter session brought change : the lectures and demonstrations ceased for a time,[1] and

amid the lower ranks of society. He was employed by his brother to cater for the dissecting-room, in the course of which employment he became a great favourite with that certainly not too respectable class of persons the resurrection-men ; and one of the amusements in which he took special pleasure, was to mingle with the gods in the shilling gallery, for the purpose of assisting to damn the productions of unhappy authors, an office in which he is said to have displayed peculiar tact and vigour." (Ottley.)

[1] " I have always given two courses of lectures every winter, each course lasting about three months. The first, and what is called the Autumn course, is finished before New Year's Day ; and the second,

JOHN HUNTER

William Hunter set his brother's steps along fresh paths. He obtained leave from Cheselden for John to see something of the practice at Chelsea Hospital. Cheselden was now more than sixty years old; his name was famous both in England and on the Continent; his love of art, his courtesy, gentleness, and sympathy made his pupils devoted to him.[1] John Hunter probably got some practical work entrusted to him—the dressing and bandaging of wounds, and what is called minor surgery. He followed Cheselden in the summers of 1749 and 1750, and to the end of his career; for the master had an attack of paralysis in 1751, and died the year after. Therefore, in 1751, John Hunter became a surgeon's pupil at St. Bartholomew's Hospital, where Percivall Pott was rising to that zenith of success whence Cheselden had just declined. He walked the wards, and was present at grave operations: which things a student may do without much profit; but it was his privilege to go straight from one good master to another, and to see the simplicity of treatment, and avoidance of

---

called the Spring course, begins about the 20th of January." (William Hunter.)

[1] "Cheselden's manners were exceedingly kind and gentle, and notwithstanding the extensive practice he had enjoyed, he always, before an operation, felt sick at the thoughts of the pain he was about to inflict. . . . He displayed considerable taste in the fine arts; he was fond of poetry, and an intimate friend of Pope; he had also made architecture his study, and it was from his plans that Putney Bridge, and the former Surgeons' Hall in the Old Bailey, were erected." (Ottley.) He was born in 1688, and died April 10, 1752.

THE TWO BROTHERS

officious interference, which made Pott so great in surgery. And when the winter of 1751–52 was over, he took a holiday; went home to Long Calderwood—if that can be home where neither father nor mother are still living to meet a man—and brought his sister Dorothea back with him to London. It was in the autumn of this year, 1752, that he made what William Hunter claimed for him as a new discovery in anatomy: of this and other discoveries achieved by John during his work in the dissecting-rooms, and of the claims and counter-claims that arose over them, some sort of account is given later in this chapter.

The year 1753 passed without changing the even course of the life of the brothers together. In 1754 John Hunter was now so set on surgery that he must attach himself to some hospital once and for all, in the hope of becoming at last a member of the staff.[1] Early in the year he entered as a surgeon's pupil at St. George's Hospital, within whose walls he was afterward to serve the hospital as surgeon for twenty-five years.

In 1755, William Hunter had a further plan to ensure the full success of his brother's life. He per-

[1] " His prospect of obtaining the situation of surgeon to the Chelsea was too uncertain and too remote to be calculated on ; and at St. Bartholomew's it would have been necessary for him to serve an apprenticeship of five years to one of the surgeons, which at his age and with his occupations was quite out of the question. Fortunately, no such obstacle offered itself at St. George's." (Ottley.)

JOHN HUNTER

suaded him to go for a time to Oxford;[1] and Mr. D'Arcy Power, whose knowledge of all things relating to John Hunter is unequalled, found not long ago the entry of his name in the matriculation list of June 5th—"Johannes Hunter, ex aula santæ maræ virginis Arm. Fil."—thus he wrote it himself as a freshman; his first opportunity in Oxford of showing his contempt for good Latin. Mr. Power believes that he left Oxford after less than two months' residence. Next year he took his name off the books; he had indeed "cracked the scheme." We need not be tragical over the matter; nor did this failure to see any advantage in Oxford shake William's faith in him. Already, in 1754, the brothers were almost on an equality in the school: John had to give some of the lectures, and to lecture if William should be called away to a patient.[2]

In May, 1756, John Hunter was appointed sole house-surgeon at St. George's Hospital; but he held this most delightful office for five months only, and resigned it in September.[3] We do not know the

[1] He entered at St. Mary's Hall as a gentleman commoner, thus escaping his matriculation examination. He lodged outside the Hall. See Mr. J. B. Bailey's Catalogue of the Exhibition of Hunterian Relics at the Royal College of Surgeons, 1893.

[2] Four years later, in 1758, the elder brother proposed that they should enter into partnership; but this plan was not carried out.

[3] "To my own knowledge I can speak it, that the period of five months' duration at the hospital in the office of house-surgeon is the shortest which can be found in the unerring journals of hospitals. The usual time for the residence of a house-surgeon is generally twelve months, but sometimes it has been extended to two years." (Jesse Foot, 1794.)

reason of his resignation, and not even Jesse Foot can find any evidence that it was Hunter's fault. Probably he could not bear to be away from his work at the school.

All this time he was only laying the foundations of the vast extent of his real work that was yet to come. Human anatomy was taking its place in his mind as but a part of all anatomy; he must know the whole animal world, every living structure in it; must dissect everything, noting all different forms and arrangements of the organs, each method of nature to adapt them to the necessities of life. He was now, in 1757, twenty-nine years old—Darwin's age when he happened to read "Malthus on Population." Thus far Darwin and Hunter, in so many ways alike, went both of them along the same highroad; here the road divides, at a narrow angle. Hunter went forward from human anatomy to all anatomy and physiology, and from these to medicine and surgery; from all of them together to profound study of life, alike in health and in disease, in all structures, at all stages.

Of his work about this time in general anatomy and physiology, Everard Home says:—

"It was not his intention to make dissections of particular animals, but to institute an inquiry into the various organisations by which the functions of life are performed, that he might thereby acquire some knowledge of general principles. This, I believe, had never been before attempted, or certainly had never been carried far into execution. So eagerly did Mr. Hunter attach himself to comparative anatomy, that he sought by every means in his power the opportunities of prosecuting it with advantage. He applied to the keeper of wild beasts in the Tower for the bodies of those which died there, and he made similar applications to the men who showed wild beasts. He purchased all rare animals which came in his way; and these, with such others as were presented to him by his friends, he entrusted to the showmen to keep till they died, the better to encourage them to assist him in his labours."

Ill health compelled him to take for a season some active occupation less unwholesome than demonstration and dissection. In 1759 he had inflammation of the lungs, attributed to overwork in the rooms, and in 1760 he was advised to go abroad, " having complaints in his breast, which threatened to be consumptive." He could not neglect this warning, for his brother James had died of consumption; and in October he was appointed a staff-surgeon in the army, by Mr. Adair,[1] then Inspector-General of Hospitals. The appointment gave him change of work, a voyage, and abundance of surgery; like Ambroise Paré, he began his practice with gunshot wounds. Early in 1761 he

[1] Robert Adair, born 1711, became a member of the Company of Barbers and Surgeons in 1738; was with the army at the siege of Quebec. Became surgeon to Chelsea Hospital, and Surgeon-General of the Army; died 1790.

went with the fleet under General Hodgson and Commodore Keppel to Belleisle, a small island off the west coast of France, which was captured after a short siege. The next year brought war with Spain, and he was a staff-surgeon on the expedition to protect the frontier of Portugal, then allied with England. With the end of 1762 came peace; and in May, 1763, he returned to London, took a house in Golden Square, and started practice as a surgeon. He was already thirty-five years old. "He found himself, in point of fortune, better than nothing by his half-pay; that enabled him to pay his house rent and some other necessaries requisite ever for those who sit down in practice waiting for patients."

These two years with the army produced the last part of Hunter's magnificent "Treatise on the Blood, Inflammation, and Gunshot Wounds," and some of his physiological observations on digestion, and on the organ of hearing in fishes. The treatise was the final work of his life, written thirty years after he had served at Belleisle and in the Peninsula; it was in the press when he died, and was published a year later, a quarto of 575 pages. The chapters on gunshot wounds are but a small portion of the book, only forty-five pages altogether. It is plain that he had seen both naval and military warfare :—

"The effects of cannon-balls on different parts of the ship, either the containing parts, as the hull of the ship itself, or the contained, are the principal causes of wounds in the sailor; for a cannon-ball must go through the timbers of the ship before it can do more execution than simply as a ball (which makes it a spent ball), and which splinters the inside of the ship very considerably, and moves other bodies in the ship."

The observations on the arrest of digestion by hibernation, and on the sense of hearing in fishes, are two good examples, out of a vast number, of his simplicity of method, wherever it was possible to be simple :—

"At Belleisle, in the beginning of the winter 1761-62, I conveyed worms and pieces of meat down the throats of lizards when they were going into winter quarters, keeping them afterwards in a cool place. On opening them at different periods I always found the substances, which I had introduced, entire, and free from any alteration : sometimes they were in the stomach ; at other times they had passed into the intestine ; and some of the lizards that were preserved alive voided them towards the spring, with but very little alteration in their structure." . . .

"In the year 1762, when I was in Portugal, I observed in a nobleman's garden, near Lisbon, a small fish-pond full of different kinds of fish. The bottom was level with the ground, the pond having been made by forming a bank all round, and had a shrubbery close to it. Whilst I lay on the bank observing the fish swimming about, I desired a gentleman who was with me to take a loaded gun and fire it from behind the shrubs. The moment the report was made, the fish seemed to be all of one mind, for they vanished instantaneously, raising a cloud of mud from the bottom."

Some letters that he wrote from abroad to his brother are put at the end of this chapter. Jesse Foot, who raked together all the gossip against him, says that he fell foul of his colleagues in the Peninsula.[1]

William Hunter, meanwhile, was hard at work in London. It is said that he never left town, from the time that he went to Long Calderwood in 1751 to the time of his death in 1783—save to see some patient in the country. He never married, he had no country-house; he looks, in his portraits, a fastidious fine gentleman; but he worked till he dropped, and he lectured when he was dying. His school was at its zenith, and he gave his whole mind to it: he stood high above the men of his time for the charm and eloquence of his lectures; he held two hospital appointments, and his private practice was one of the largest in London. Moreover, he must be doing literary work

---

[1] "He had scarcely arrived at Portugal, before he excited an uneasiness among the faculty, which their situations had never experienced before. He turned the common intercourses of social good humour into suspicious tauntings of jealousy: he created a faction and a consequent disgust. This brought on an explanation from one who was his senior in the army by ten years;—from one who had been a faithful follower of the Duke of Cumberland, and had dressed his wounds in battle. He was roused to draw his sword upon John Hunter, which was sheathed without the quarrel being reconciled—for what reconciliation can remove suspicion? The confirmation of this I am not disposed to doubt, but some there are who may: those I will assist as far as it is in my power by assuring them—*that the manly veteran Tomkins, of Park Place, is very capable of explaining the fact.*"

—monographs on matters of pathology—and already, so early as 1751, he had made a beginning of that magnificent Atlas of the "Anatomy of the Gravid Uterus," not published till 1775, which is perhaps the greatest book that has yet been written on this special subject.

For all this, he found time to proclaim and protect his brother's discoveries in anatomy.[1] In 1762, the year John was in the Peninsula, William Hunter published his "Medical Commentaries. Part I.": surely one of the strangest books that a physician or a surgeon ever wrote.[2] From beginning to end, it is an incessant attack on those who discovered what the brothers also discovered; every device of italic type, notes of exclamation, and long quotations, interrogation and interjection, heavy sarcasm, charges of stupidity, falsehood, and flagrant theft—all these things make the book, and there is nothing else in it, hardly one line that

[1] "It is certain that Dr. Hunter took every opportunity of acknowledging to his audience the obligations he owed to his absent brother. My friend Dr. Cogan, who, happily for all who share his acquaintance, lives to relate transactions of more than half a century past, informs me that in the winter of 1762-3, Dr. Hunter would frequently introduce in his lectures—'In this I am only my brother's interpreter'—'I am simply the demonstrator of this discovery; it was my brother's.' Dr. Cogan adds, 'The frequency of such expressions naturally inspired all his pupils with admiration of Mr. Hunter's skill in anatomical researches, and of the Doctor's ingenuous conduct.'" (Adams.)

[2] "Medical Commentaries. Part I. Containing a Plain and Direct Answer to Professor Monro, jun., Interspersed with Remarks on the Structure, Functions, and Diseases of Several Parts of the Human Body. By William Hunter, M.D. London, 1762." Small quarto, 113 pp. With a Supplement, 1764, 33 pp.

THE TWO BROTHERS

is quiet. It was the method of controversy fashionable in his time, full of sound and fury. The points at issue lay between the brothers on the one side, and the Monroes of Edinburgh on the other side; and to these disputes was added a controversy with Percivall Pott. The claims and counter-claims must be put here; but this is not the place to decide, even if it were possible, between the disputants.

1. *The discovery of the lachrymal ducts in man.* This was not so much a discovery as a demonstration. It was common knowledge that many animals have them, and it was no new thing to try to find them in the human body. In 1747, during his first course of anatomical lectures, William Hunter succeeded in demonstrating them. Dr. Alexander Monro, junior, gave a similar demonstration of them, at Edinburgh, for the first time, in 1753; but when he published an account of it, he made no mention of William Hunter, though he had by that time attended a course of his lectures. "Is it not very singular," says William Hunter, "that he should have made so many discoveries in the year 1753 at Edinburgh, and that all of them should have been published before that time at my lectures in London? Is it not pretty plain how he came by them, when we are informed, that every winter there were some students at Edinburgh who had attended my lectures; and about this very time some of these gentlemen belonged to a society, of which he was a member, instituted by the students for

talking and disputing upon medical subjects ? Does it not agree with and support this insinuation, that he published such things as his own, after he had heard them from my mouth before a numerous audience, without doing me the justice of putting my name into a marginal note ? I am resolved to take no further notice of him."

2. *The discovery of the tubuli seminiferi.* Here again the question is not of discovery, but of successful demonstration. Wherever there is a duct, there must necessarily be minute sacs or tubules, secretory cavities of some kind, opening into it : the difficulty was to inject mercury into the duct so skilfully that it should fill the tubules and define them without rupturing them. This delicate bit of work was done by the brothers in 1752, and by Dr. Alexander Monro, at Edinburgh, two or three weeks later. William Hunter vehemently asserted that the news of his own success must have reached Monro in some underhand way. Dr. Garrow, a physician practising at Barnet, had been writing to Monro, and must have told him the news ; and Monro must have stolen the discovery. "I wish it were possible to prove that he did not learn it of me at second hand : I wish it for his sake, because it would clear him, and take nothing from me. But considering that letter of Dr. Garrow, and the constant intercourse between the schools of anatomy at London and Edinburgh, the presumption must always be against him." William Hunter got six medical men

to write letters, which he published, to prove the exact date at which he showed the injected specimens to his class: he claimed priority as eagerly as if he had discovered the law of gravitation. Dr. Donald Monro answered for his brother, that Haller had done much the same thing at Göttingen in 1751, and had published it before William Hunter had done it; and that the name of Hunter was hardly a household word in Edinburgh. "What Dr. Hunter means by saying he published this discovery before my brother, is what I do not comprehend; if he means by publishing, showing it in his private colleges, he puts a meaning upon the word *publishing* different from what I understand by it; for I dissected five years for my father, from 1745 to 1750, and had in the winter constantly numbers of the pupils about me, and was intimate with many of them, especially of the English young gentlemen: yet while I remained at Edinburgh, I never could know one thing Dr. Hunter was doing: and since I have been in London, I have not heard more, except some few things relative to the present dispute, and what I heard accidentally from the Doctor himself in private conversation."

3. *The discoveries relating to congenital hernia.* In 1755, Haller in his "Opuscula Pathologica" suggested that the form of hernia called "congenital" was not an ordinary hernia that had undergone secondary changes, but was due to a persistent embryonic state of the parts concerned in its production. William

JOHN HUNTER

Hunter read Haller's work that same year, and urged his brother to make a whole series of dissections of the parts. This John did during the winter of 1755–56: and in April, 1756, William Hunter, in the course of his lectures, gave a general account of these observations. A few months later, Percivall Pott published his book on hernia. Though he had not read Haller, he gave much the same account of the embryonic arrangement of the parts, and of congenital hernia; saying, "This has always appeared to me to be the case." John Hunter went on with his dissections, to such good purpose that William, in the autumn course of 1756, was able to demonstrate the whole matter in a complete series of preparations. Then, in November, Percivall Pott called one morning at Covent Garden, saw John Hunter, and went over the specimens with him. Next March, he published a pamphlet of forty pages on the subject; in which neither of the brothers was so much as named. It is no wonder that William Hunter was furious. "Mr. Pott called at my lecture-rooms in the morning, because he knew I was there only in the evening. . . . His treatise hardly contained one new idea; it was what any of my pupils might have written, and yet neither my brother's name nor mine was mentioned: I complained of this at my lectures. . . . In this production of Mr. P., the doctrine being transplanted from its native soil, and nursed up in the dark, was imperfect; the pamphlet was a *time-serving* composition, which was hurried into the world, to snatch the only possible moment for raising reputation. . . . I complained of him by name, in the most open manner, in my lecture, to about an *hundred gentlemen*." Percivall Pott answered that William Hunter had no right thus to abuse him in public to a set of people who could not possibly know anything of the matter; that he himself had stolen nothing either from Haller or from the Hunters, but had worked the subject out for himself, with one of his dressers at St. Bartholomew's Hospital; that John Hunter had shown him only one preparation of the parts, and had said nothing about congenital hernia. The brothers answered him, William with angry rhetoric, John with a plain statement of all that he remembered of Percivall Pott's visit to the rooms. It is impossible to determine the rights of the case; but the dissections that John Hunter made, and his account of them, are work of the very highest order, patient, skilful, and original.

4. *The discovery of the absorbent system.* Here was a new truth of vast importance, second only to Harvey's discovery of the circulation of the blood; it changed the whole character of medical science and practice. That the lacteals, which carry food-products into the blood, were absorbent vessels, men knew already; but they had not realised that the whole body, every organ and tissue of it, is penetrated, and drained of all excess of fluid, by a special system of interstitial spaces and canals—the lymphatic vessels,

with their glands—discharging the fluid back into the general circulation. They had believed that this work of absorption was done by the veins, and that the lymphatic canals were connected with the terminal branches of the arterial system. But William Hunter, in the very first course of his anatomical lectures, 1746-47, taught the true nature of the absorbent system, and brought arguments and preparations to support his teaching. He spoke with some reserve and uncertainty, his views were not yet confirmed by experiment, and he did not commit himself to print. Still, he taught the new knowledge year after year. In 1752-53, young Alexander Monro, at Edinburgh, after much thought and many experiments, arrived at the same truth, and would have published his results, in his thesis for the M.D. degree of Edinburgh, but they were too lengthy; so he gave a sort of abstract of them, and a promise of more. The thesis was published in October, 1755; a copy was sent to William Hunter; then its author came to London, and attended William Hunter's lectures, 1755-56; then, in the summer of 1756, he went to Berlin to study, and there, in the beginning of 1757, published a treatise, "De venis lymphaticis valvulosis." "And though he knew," says William Hunter, "from my own mouth, in the presence of a great number of students, that I had taught the same doctrine, and supported it by the *very same* arguments several years before, he did not mention my name, not even in a marginal note.

THE TWO BROTHERS

. . . Upon inquiry, I found that manuscripts of my lectures were very common among the students at Edinburgh about the time that Professor Monro pretends to have made his discoveries. That he should expose himself thus to the world! That his father should suffer him to do so!"

The fierceness of the quarrel was in proportion to the value of the discovery; all three Monroes, the father and his sons, threw themselves into it against the Hunters. On his way back from Berlin to Edinburgh, the offender called on William Hunter in Jermyn Street to make his peace with him, but did not find him at home. "He called upon me indeed at my house in Jermyn Street, but it was *when I was reading my lecture at Covent Garden;* that is, *when he was certain I was not at home.*"

To prove that he had described the absorbent system before Monro, William Hunter published thirteen letters from old pupils who had attended his lectures; to prove that Monro had called at his house knowing he was out, he published an affidavit from his own butler. Monro's father replied on the whole case, asserting that his son had stolen nothing from any notes of William Hunter's lectures, but that the latter had stolen what was best in his lectures from young Monro's thesis. Later, in 1758–59, John Hunter made a series of very valuable experiments and dissections, which established the whole truth about the absorbent system; and he was preparing to carry his

JOHN HUNTER

work yet further, when his health gave way, and he joined the expedition to Belleisle.

These famous disputes of the Hunters with the Monroes and with Percivall Pott must not be taken too seriously: it was the fashion of the time to conduct every controversy, after the example of Dr. Johnson, as though it were a criminal case at the Old Bailey. Yet it is evident that William, more than other men, was proud of his success, irritable, and suspicious; that John, less apt for rhetoric, was not less obdurate over facts, or less conscious of his strength; and that each of them alike would have his rights, and would hold it a point of honour to fight against the least infringement of them. Therefore, since it was neither sentiment nor temperament that bound the brothers together, nor anything else but work, they would break the bond between them, so soon as they began to dispute over their work; and the very vehemence with which they had fought side by side, against men who claimed the discoveries that they had made working side by side, would at last thrust them apart, whenever they should both lay claim to the same discovery.

For the remainder of this chapter, some short account must be given of the latter half of William Hunter's life, the final estrangement of the brothers, and the death of William Hunter in 1783.[1] He

[1] "About ten years before his death, his health was so much impaired that, fearing he might soon become unfit for the fatigues of his profession,

remained faithful to his "darling London"; and consoled himself for his loneliness with the fine arts, and with hard work. He made a yearly allowance to his sister Dorothea, after her husband's death in 1778; she and her daughters, Joanna and Agnes, had his house for their home; her son Matthew was treated as his own son. He had the friendship of Reynolds, Gainsborough, Hogarth, Johnson,[1] and all the great men of his time; he stood well with the King, who appointed him in 1764 Physician Extraordinary to the Queen, and in 1768 Professor of Anatomy to the new Royal Academy; and he had an immense practice. He spent his money on science and art; he gathered for himself, and gave to the nation, that most wonderful art-collection which alone would perpetuate his name: pictures, portraits, engravings, books, manuscripts, coins, and curiosities. There are more than 12,000 books, with specimens of almost every press since the introduction of printing; almost every work in classic

he began to think of retiring to Scotland. With this view he requested his friends Dr. Cullen and Dr. Baillie to look out for a pleasant estate for him. A considerable one, and such as they thought would be agreeable to him, was offered for sale about that time in the neighbourhood of Alloa. A description of it was sent to him, and met with his approbation. The price was agreed on, and the bargain supposed to be concluded. But when the title-deeds of the estate came to be examined by Dr. Hunter's counsel in London, they were found defective, and he was advised not to complete the purchase. After this, he found the expenses of his museum increase so fast that he laid aside all thoughts of retiring from practice." (Simmons).

[1] In the Library of the Royal College of Surgeons, there is a letter from Dr. Johnson to him, thanking him for his promise to present to the King a copy of Dr. Johnson's "Journey to the Hebrides."

JOHN HUNTER

and foreign literature known to exist previous to the sixteenth century. The coins and medals are of incalculable value: a hundred years ago, the trustees of the British Museum offered £20,000 for only a portion of them. It was one of the finest private collections in the world. There are six hundred manuscripts: gems, minerals, corals and shells, specimens in natural history and geology.[1]

Nevertheless, neither practice nor art was the ruling passion of his life, but anatomy; and it is no wonder that men have put him equal with Vesalius. So early as 1765, he offered £7,000 to found a central school of anatomy in London; he would give the money at once, and at some later date his books and specimens: "My library has already cost me between £3,000 and £4,000; and my anatomical museum is of more worth to the public, because they are things that cannot be bought;" he would build and enrich the school, if Government would give him a site. His offer was refused. Then, in 1768, he built himself a house, lecturing-theatre, dissecting-rooms, and museum, in Great Windmill Street;[2] here he worked hard

[1] This magnificent collection, and his anatomical museum, he left to the University of Glasgow. A full account of them is given in Dr. Mather's delightful book, "Two Great Scotsmen," and in Professor Young's "Address on the Hunterian Library." Glasgow, 1897.

[2] "In this building, besides a handsome amphitheatre and other convenient apartments for lectures and dissections, there was one magnificent room fitted up with great elegance and propriety as a museum." (Simmons.) When the school in Great Windmill Street, long after his death, came to an end, the buildings were at one time used as a restaurant;

THE TWO BROTHERS

till he died, dissecting, lecturing, and collecting specimens and preparations. In 1775, he published his Atlas, the work of thirty years. "There was, perhaps, never a book published by any physician, on which longer and severer labour was bestowed." In its preface, he spoke in general terms of the help that his brother had given him—"whose accuracy in anatomical researches is so well known that to omit this opportunity of thanking him would be in some measure to disregard the future reputation of the work itself"—but made no mention of any special knowledge he had learned from him.

The passion for anatomy that had united the brothers was now to separate them; yet the blow did not fall, for some reason not known to us, for five years. Then, early in 1780, John Hunter communicated to the Royal Society a short paper "On the Structure of the Placenta." Its first paragraph is a direct challenge to his brother, and shows that a dispute had already taken place between them:—

"The connexion between the mother and foetus in the human subject has, in every age in which science has been cultivated, called forth the attention of the anatomist, the physiologist, and even the philosopher; but both that connexion, and the structure of the parts

---

now, they form the back-part of the Lyric Theatre, and the stage-door is where the bodies used to be taken into the house for dissection. He had thought of living in Whitehall, but gave up this plan in favour of Great Windmill Street. The site that he desired for his Central School was where the National Gallery now stands.

which form the connexion, were unknown till about the year 1754. The subject is certainly most interesting, and the discovery important; and it is my intention, in the following pages, to give such an account of it as I hope may be acceptable to the public; while, at the same time, I establish my own claim to the discovery. But that I may not seem to arrogate to myself more merit than I am entitled to, let me, in justice to another person, relate what follows."

This other person was not William Hunter, but Dr. Mackenzie, Dr. Smellie's assistant, who procured and prepared the specimen which John Hunter dissected, in May, 1754. "The examination was made in Dr. Mackenzie's presence, and in the presence of several other gentlemen, whose names I have now forgotten. . . . It may be suspected by some (but none I hope to whom I have the pleasure of being known) that I am not doing Dr. Mackenzie justice, and am perhaps suppressing some part of that share of the discovery to which he is entitled. This idea (if ever it should arise) I may probably not be able to remove; but I hope it will also be seen that I myself have given rise to it; believing, if I had been so inclined, that I might have suppressed Dr. Mackenzie's name altogether without ever running the hazard of being detected. I was indeed so tenacious of my claim to the discovery, that I wrote this account in Dr. Mackenzie's lifetime, with a design to publish it; and often communicated my intentions to Dr. George Fordyce, who I knew was very intimate with the Doctor, in consequence of both teaching in the same place, and making many experiments together; therefore he is a kind of collateral witness, that what I now publish is the same account which I gave in Dr. Mackenzie's lifetime."

John Hunter goes on to describe how he dissected and demonstrated the preparation: "But the company, prejudiced in favour of former theories, combated my opinion. . . . I returned home in the evening, and communicating what I had discovered to my brother, Dr. Hunter, who at first treated it and me with good-humoured raillery; but on going with me to Dr. Mackenzie's he was soon convinced of the fact. Some of the parts were given to him, which he afterwards showed at his lectures, and probably they still remain in his collection. . . . The facts being now ascertained and universally acknowledged, I consider myself as having a just claim to the discovery of the structure of the placenta and its communication with the uterus, together with the use arising from such structure and communication."

He mentions William Hunter's discovery of the decidua reflexa. He makes allusion to the Atlas, "that very accurate and elaborate work which Dr. Hunter has published on the Gravid Uterus, in which he has minutely described and accurately delineated the parts, without mentioning the mode of discovery." And he quotes some manuscript notes, taken by one of the audience at his brother's lectures in 1755–56, to prove that William Hunter, even then, a year after the discovery of the placental structure, neither spoke of it nor understood the meaning of it.

Time has not softened the ugliness of this astonishing communication to the Royal Society. It was read, but not published in the Transactions. We look for some sort of excuse for it, and find only such gossip as makes it worse—that William Hunter had disapproved, nine years earlier, of John Hunter's marriage; that they had disputed over the possession of certain anatomical preparations; that John Hunter's judgment had been weakened by ill-health. We are still left wholly unable to see why he waited twenty-six years, and then, when he was fifty-two years old, raised a storm over a dissection that he had made when he was twenty-six.

William Hunter forthwith wrote to the Royal Society; then John wrote. I give the letters at length.[1] The Society refused to take up the dispute,

I.[1]

WINDMILL STREET, *Feb.* 3, 1780.

Dr. Hunter begs the favour that the Secretary to the Royal Society will read to the Society what follows.

Mr. Hunter's account of the structure of the human placenta, explaining the connexion and circulation between the mother and fœtus in utero, which was read at the last meeting of the Royal Society, informs us that it was a discovery which he made with Dr. Mackenzie, and that it was not claimed by me. The Society will be sensible that I am reduced to the necessity of taking notice of this mistake, when they are informed of the following facts:

First. That the doctrine has been many years ago published in printed

or to publish the paper. Three years later, on Sunday, March 30, 1783, William Hunter died, sixty-four years old; and said, as he was dying, "If I had strength enough to hold a pen, I would write how easy and pleasant a thing it is to die." On Saturday, March 15th, he had taken to his bed, after some days of illness from gout. On Thursday, the 20th, he must give the introductory address of his course of lectures on the operations of surgery; he would not be advised, gave the lecture, then fainted from exhaustion, and was taken home. On the 22nd, he told Mr. Combe that during the night he had certainly had a paralytic stroke; and now John Hunter was allowed to do him those services that a paralysed man may need of a surgeon. His mind remained clear; the last

books as my discovery, and had been communicated as such by myself. See Baron Haller, for instance, in the second part of the eighth volume (p. 220) of his great Physiology in quarto, printed thirteen or fourteen years ago.

Secondly. Besides treating of it as my own discovery in my lectures on the subject, I have always done so, for many years past, in the very first lecture of my course, which is the most public of all, because the door is then open to every person whose curiosity prompts him to be present.

In the third place, occasionally in what I have printed, and in my lectures, I hope I have not overlooked opportunities of doing justice to Mr Hunter's great merits, and of acknowledging that he had been an excellent assistant to me in this and in many other pursuits. By doing so, I always felt an inward gratification, shall I call it, or pride? I have given him all the little anatomical knowledge that I could communicate, and put him into the very best situation that I could, for becoming what this Society has, for some time, known him to be. May it be presumed then that I stand possessed of the discovery in question, till proofs shall be brought to dispossess me? I shall most willingly submit to the pleasure of

words of his life were those that he spoke in praise of the ease and pleasantness of his death. He did not make his brother his executor, and left nothing to him; neither money, nor the care of the museum, nor the old home at Long Calderwood.

I.

From John Hunter to William Hunter.

DEAR BROTHER,—I wrote to you a good while ago and should have wrote often if anything had hapen'd concerning our affairs here worth writing, we are all here very impatient for Letters; none have come to this Island these five or six weeks; but we are here full of news coming round by Guernsey, &c. We talk of going home, and then to go out upon another expedition, viz., to Martinico, if there is anything in

the Society; if they signify an unwillingness that this emulation (shall I call it?) should go on, I shall acquiesce, and be silent. If curiosity, justice, or the laws and practice of the Society should incline the Council to seek out and determine upon the merits, I shall be equally ready to obey their commands. And if it should appear reasonable to them, I would first beg to know the grounds of Mr. Hunter's claim, as I am too well acquainted with his abilities not to think that he must be able to support his claim by something that I am ignorant of. And if I should receive that satisfaction, I shall immediately show that I am more tenacious of truth than even of anatomical discoveries. But if that information should not alter my thoughts on the question, I shall show to the satisfaction of the Society, if I can at all judge of my own employments and pursuits, that my pretensions arise out of a long series of observations and experiments made with a view to the discovery in question; that it was not a random conjecture, a lucky thought, or accidental occasion, but a persevering pursuit for twelve or thirteen years at least, the progress of which

it, I would beg of you to see if I could possibly avoid it, and be put upon some land service as the Sea plays the Devil with me. I would rather stay here in this place (if a surgeon is to be left with the Troops) than go to the west or east Indies; but if there was no chance of going to either, I would come home with the forces that comes home; as I can have it in my power to do either, I'll beg that you'll inquire of Mr. Adair, with my most Humble respects. I don't suppose that a pourvaiour (purveyor) will be left here, as no hospital will be left, but this is only conjecture. Mr. Adair knows these things best.

I should like to know how anatomy is to go on this was always publicly known here, and admits of the most circumstantial proof.

WILLIAM HUNTER.

II.

To the President of the Royal Society.

JERMYN STREET, *Feb.* 17, 1780.

SIR,—Though I know the constitution of the Society over which you preside too well to suppose that they will give their judgment on any subject, and respect it too much to think it a proper field for waging the war of controversy, I cannot avoid requesting you to lay before that learned body a short answer to the paper given in by my brother, Dr. Hunter; as silence on my part, after his charge, may be interpreted by my enemies into an acknowledgment that I have intentionally claimed to myself a discovery in reality his due. I am as tenacious as he is of anatomical discovery, and, I flatter myself, as tenacious also of truth. The discovery was made in the manner in which I stated it in my paper. Dr. Mackenzie had injected the subject, and being unable, as I conceived, to explain an appearance which he had found in dissecting it, sent for me. I came to him, and having examined it further, explained the appearance in question, then, for the first time, to my own satisfaction and that of Dr. Mackenzie; and in the evening of the same day, full of the discovery, I came to Dr. Hunter, and brought him with me to Dr. Mac-

winter. Let me know how Dr. Pitcairn is and Dr. Makauly, give my Compts. to them.

I forgot to ask how our sister Doritha and Mr. Baily are. Let me hear from you as soon as you can as perhaps no time is to be lost.

From your most affectionate Brother
JOHN HUNTER.

BELLEISLE *July* 11*th* 1761.

When you write let your Letter be directed to the care of some person at Plymouth as no letters comes from Portsmouth.

kenzie, to see and judge of the explanation I had given and Dr. Mackenzie had agreed to. This is my state of the fact upon which I ground my belief of myself being the author of this anatomical discovery; but as my brother thinks differently, after a period of twenty-five years, I am content to abolish all remembrance of the successions of time in the course of that day, and to suppose that Dr. Mackenzie, Dr. Hunter, and myself inspected the parts together, and made the discovery, by which means the honour of it will be divided into three, one of which I may surely be allowed to take to myself, the other two may appertain to Dr. Mackenzie and Dr. Hunter, if they choose to claim, and be content with them; though in this division we must make some reserve for the claims of several ingenious young men, at that time pupils, who were with us, and of course entitled to some proportional share in the discovery, though their present situations, settled at a distance from this town, have prevented them from getting early notice of this present claim, and of course of making application to the Society for their share. However, I may here declare that if Dr. Hunter will produce to me any claim, which I can allow, of his having discovered this anatomical fact at any period of time prior to this conference at Dr. Mackenzie's, I shall first declare, in excuse for having troubled the Society, that I was not before acquainted with it, and immediately after declare that he is entitled to the sole honour of it, at least in preference to myself.

I am, Sir,
Your much obliged, and most obedient humble Servant,
JOHN HUNTER.

THE TWO BROTHERS

II.

From John Hunter to William Hunter.

DEAR BROTHER,—I recd. yours, from General Hodgson who has rather been more free ever since, however, he is not burthend with that disposition yet. I was very Glad to hear from you, for here we seem to be a people almost distinct from the rest of the world. I am very much obliged to you for the trouble that you have been at in enquiring after my future steps that I am to take ; and shall still beg your assistance, in letting me know any news that may concern me, with your oppinion of it ; and if you should be so much hurried as not to have time to write I'll beg Mr. Pittegrew to call, to know your mind. My scheme at present is this ; If we are order'd home, and a surgeon is to stay here, I propose staying (if there is any chance of another expedition) and if I do stay, I propose applying for the deputy parveorship (purveyorship), which is ten shillings a day, and if I get that I can give my Prentice a place of five shillings a day, so that I can make it worth my while, this is my present plan.

I am very much obliged to Col. Mackinzie for his good character, but these things are all blawflum : however it is a sort of acknowledgemint of my services to him. Thank God I have succeeded in everything that I have attempted, but my practice in Gunshot wounds has been in a great Mesure different from all others, so that I have had the eyes of all the surgeons upon me, both on account of my suppos'd knowledge, and method of treatment. My fellow Creatures of the Hospital are a damn'd disagreeable set. The two Heads are as unfit for their employment, as the devil was to reign in Heaven, but more of all this hereafter. I shall be glad of hearing that you have got a good place, and a good assistant for your anatomy, likewise what you have done with Monro. There is a Gentleman here that attended Douglas at the time of the dispute, and he says that Douglas give it to you in his Lectures, but more so in his privit conversation. I wanted a letter from him on that head, but he declined it, as he had formerly been a Pupil of old Monro's, but if you think that it is a great deal to your purpose, I'll do all I can to get it. Please to give my best respects to Sr. John Haukins' family, to Drs. Pitcairn, Smollet, Pringle, and Macauly.

From your affectionate Brother
JOHN HUNTER.

BELLEISLE *Septr. 28th* 1761.

N.B.—General Hodgeson desired that any letters of mine might come over in his packet.

III.

From John Hunter to William Hunter.

DEAR BROTHER,—There is nothing here talkd of but Portugal, Mr. Smith our apothecary is appointed as one there; but no accounts of my going. If I am to leave this place I should like to go there, but should chuse to stay here, if an Hospital was to be keept, as I suppose that I shall loose my ten shilling by going (but that as it may be). I am told that our arreas are to be paid in two months. I wrote some time ago to Mr. Young about it, and now to Mr. Hope. I think that it should amount by that time to a £160 for my Prentice and myself. I hear that Dr. Blyth is to go to Portugal, I suppose that Mr. Young goes as Surgeon-General, God help the Hospital when directed by such two. I wonder who will be purveyor, for Young's commission is changed. If you can learn how things are likely to go on, I wish you would write me; or I'll order Pettigrew to call, in case your time should be taken up, which I dare say is very much the case. I have enclosed a Letter for Mr. Adair, if you think that it is a proper one, you'll be pleased to seal it and send it to him, if not there is no harm done.

From your most affectionate Brother
JOHN HUNTER.

BELLEISLE, *April* 12*th* 1762.

IV.

From John Hunter to William Hunter.

DEAR BROTHER,—I have read your answer to Monro, I think that it is just the thing that it should be. It would give me great joy to see him read it. I am very much obliged to you for your introduction of me; I think my name will live, now that it is joind with yours. Mr. Pettigrew gives me strong hope of your being imployed by the Queen. I think after all that I may come in for something. We are all busie making ready for Portugal but there seems to be no great signs. I'll refer you to Mr. Pettigrew for particulars, with regard to our situation here. I had almost forgot to mention the Medical observations, I think that they are good upon the whole, but that case of Ingham's is shurly a Lie, and I think there is too much Splutter about the coros. Sub. I am vastly pleasd with your second case of the aneurism, it is entirly new to me; the other papers of yours I in some measure knew before.

   Believe me to be dear Brother your's

       JOHN HUNTER.

BELLEISLE, *June 6th*, 1762.

v.

From John Hunter to William Hunter.

DEAR BROTHER,—When I recd. your Letter at Belleisle informing me that the Secretary at War had promised me the Deputy Directorship, I was in hopes of getting it; and when I came to Lisbon Mr. Young told me that I was the person. I had no sooner heard this, than Mr. Madox (one of our Surgeons) produces a warrent for the imployment, granted by my Lord Tyrawly; and at the same time, Lord Loudoun's promise that he should keep it. Upon enquiry, we were told by the Surgeon that it was only granted conditionaly, viz., if I came from Belleisle it was to have no effect; which shows that they knew of my being appointed, or approved of. From this declaration of the Surgeon's he was led to give up all pretentions to it, and even to write Lord Loudoun a letter to that effect; when Lord Loudoun was asked what he chused to do, he put us off till he saw Lord Tyrawly,—they met, but this meeting determined nothing : only that the person should be appointed at home by the Secretary at War, and he receive advice of it from thence.

Now as there has been so many promises of the Surgeon's to give it up, and that my Lord Tyrawly allowed him to do it; but yet it is never done; and my Lord Loudoun's leaving it to be done in London; makes me suspect, that they want to cheat me out of it, because Lord Tyrawly and the Surgeon goes home in the same ship with this Letter and (most likely) will make immediate application to the Secretary at War for a warrant, which will determine it at home. This I suspect to be their drift, and I would therefor disapoint them, by being before hand with them. From what has hapen'd in London concerning my being the person, I should suppose that I am look'd upon there as the person that has it. If this is the case, I should look upon it as an easy thing to get a warrant or an acknowledgment from the war office, that I am the person appointed; now all this must be done before Lord Tyrawly gets to London. If you could have time to wait upon Mr. Tyrwhitt, Deputy Secratory at war, and ask to see Mr. Young's return of those that were to act under him; and ask at the same time if Mr. Townsand has seen it; it proves that he approved of me by his not contradicting it, and if he has aproved of it he cannot be against granting a warrant or fixing it for me. From what I can learn, Lord Loudoun would be my friend if he would appear in it. Mr. Young is my stance friend and does everything in his power to serve me. I wish I could get it as it makes a vast difference with me here. I am Dear Brother Your &c., JOHN HUNTER.

LISBON, *July* 25 1762.

Please to direct for me at Mr. Christr. Hake's, marchant in Lisbon. You are to show Mr. Young's letter to ye Secratory.

VI.

From John Hunter to William Hunter.

DEAR BROTHER,—Nothing could give me more pleasure than seeing your advertisment in the papers, excepting a peace. I expected to have heard from you about my Directorship, therefore have done nothing in it till I should hear from you; but I am inform'd by the bye that Lord Loudoun must have a Letter from the Secretary at war before he will interfear in it. I

am now applying for Phisician, if I get that I shall be a Dr. as well as the best of you. I have attended his Lordship in all his marches, and have reason to believe that I am well with him. I should like to read a letter from you. I am Dear Brother Your's
JOHN HUNTER.

PORTALEGRA *Nov.* 16*th*.

VII.

From William Cullen to William Hunter.

EDINBR., 29*th Augst.*, 1776.

MY DEAR FRIEND,—I have wished to have your opinion on many subjects, and if I was near you I should be very troublesome. Your distance has hitherto saved you, but I must now break thro that obstacle... You will perceive that I have decided many controversies which you are a much better judge of than I am, and I expect your opinion, without reserve... I am this day to pay my last duty to David Hume, and you may believe with great concern. By Dr. Black's nonchalance there has been no dissection, so that I can tell your brother John nothing more exactly concerning his disease. Believe me to be with great affection,

My dear Friend, Yours &c., &c.,
WILLIAM CULLEN.

JOHN HUNTER

VIII.

From William Cullen to William Hunter.

EDIN., 17th Septr., 1776.

. . . He (Mr. Hume) was truly an example *des grands hommes qui sont morts en plaisantant.* Not many days before his death, a friend found him reading, and upon enquiring what was the book, Mr. Hume told him it was Lucian, and that he had been just reading the dialogue entitled καταπλοῦς, in which Megapentes arriving on the banks of the Styx urges many pleas for being allowed to return for some time to the world. Mr. Hume said the fancy had struck him to think what pleas he himself might offer upon such an occasion. He thought he might say that he had been very busily employed in making his countrymen wiser, and particularly in delivering them from the Christian superstition, but that he had not yet compleated that great work . . . These are a few particulars which may perhaps appear trifling, but to me no particulars seem trifling that relate to so great a man. It is perhaps from trifles that we can best distinguish the tranquillity and chearfulness of the Philosopher at a time when the most part of mankind are under disquiet, anxiety, and sometimes horror. I consider the sacrifice of the Cock as a more certain evidence of the tranquillity of Socrates than his discourse on Immortality.

III.

LONDON, 1763-1771.—GOLDEN SQUARE: EARL'S COURT

"Well, Lynn, I must go and earn this damned guinea, or I shall be sure to want it to-morrow."

JOHN HUNTER, when he came back from the Peninsula in 1763, and started practice in Golden Square, was thirty-five, and had thirty years more to live. First came the years of waiting for practice; that rise from the river of Time like the lean kine in Pharaoh's dream—"poor and very ill favoured and leanfleshed, such as I never saw in all the land of Egypt for badness." There were many difficulties in his way. He was only one more surgeon in London, against men of greater experience: and the good things of practice were in the hands of the leaders—Percivall Pott above all: Bromfield and Cæsar Hawkins, of St. George's Hospital; Sharp and Warner, of Guy's Hospital. He had no hospital appointment; he had already lived twelve years in London, but in all that time had not published one word of writing: then, for two more years, he had disappeared out of England, his place in the school had been filled by Mr. Hewson, and things had gone on well without him. He had not the art of making patients; and his age was not altogether in his favour, for people would ask what he had been doing all this time.

Moreover, his passion for scientific work delayed his success as a surgeon; it dominated the opinions which men had of him, and made him impatient of the common things of practice. To the profession, he was known as a good anatomist, subordinate to his brother; he had given twelve years to a science which they considered not essential to surgery, still less to medicine; and had made some original observations, that his brother had lately published in his Medical Commentaries. To the people round Golden Square, he was a zealous student of the human body, who might or might not restore you to health, but would certainly wish to anatomize you if he failed. And to himself, practice appeared subordinate to anatomy and pathology; and the fees that he made by it must all be spent on scientific work. "To this object was devoted every hour that he could spare from his daily avocations, or snatch from the time allotted by others to sleep . . . To witness an interesting or extraordinary case, he would take any trouble, or go almost any distance, without a chance of pecuniary recompense; but to the daily routine of practice he always returned

LONDON, 1763-1771

unwillingly; and even when he had acquired a lucrative and extensive business, he valued it only as affording him the means of pursuing his favourite studies." And then Ottley quotes that brave saying about the guinea, which is put at the head of this chapter—words Hunter often used, as he laid aside his dissecting instruments, and went out to see a patient.

"What happened to John Hunter, happens to every surgeon in the beginning; there was not employment enough furnished by the practical art, to fill up the active hours of the day. . . . He opened a room for dissections, and demonstrated subjects to his pupils: he began to make preparations upon his own account. . . . He had not at this time exacted those rigid severities of temperance to which he was observed to adhere at his latter part of life. John Hunter at this time, and for some time after, was a companionable man: he associated in company, drank his bottle, told his story, and laughed with others." (Jesse Foot.)

That he might study living animals, both by experiment and by observation of their habits, he must have a foothold outside London; he found it "about two miles from London, near Brompton, at a place called Earl's Court." Here, in 1764, he bought two acres of land, and built a small house to suit himself. It so expressed his work and character that the accounts of it suggest something endowed with life; and the news of its demolition, ten years ago, came like the announcement of a man's death. It was not only alive, but highly organised, a most complex or heterogeneous structure; a farm, a menagerie, an institute of anatomy and physiology, and a villa decorated in the fashion of the period.

"Nobody of common curiosity could have passed this original cottage without being obliged to inquire to whom it belonged. By observing the back of the house, a lawn was found, stocked with fowls and animals of the strangest selection in nature, as if it had been another repository belonging to Brooks; and in the front there were to be seen four figures in lead or stone representing Lions, two in a form *passant* placed upon the parapet, and on the ground two more *couchant*, guarding the double flight of steps leading to the vestibule. On the sides of the area were seen two pyramidal collections of shells, of a very contracted base, and mean height, each of them seeming to conceal a subterraneous entrance to a Golgotha. Over the front door was presented the mouth of a crocodile gaping tremendously wide. Here it was, that he pastured those Buffaloes which he so lately as in 1792 put into harness and trotted through the streets of London; not judging, that he might have been fairly outrivalled by a showman's Dromedary."[1] . . .

[1] This, of course, was written by Jesse Foot; a year after Hunter died. The *Morning Post* of August 30, 1793, only a few weeks before his death, says, "In the gardens of Mr. John Hunter, surgeon, at Earl's Court, are seen buffaloes, rams, and sheep from Turkey, and a shawl-goat from the East Indies, all feeding together in the greatest harmony;

LONDON, 1763–1771

At the east end of the grounds, near the gates, was an artificial mound of earth, having an opening in its side, which led into three small vaults or cellars beneath it. On the top of the mound, was a little rampart of bricks and tiles, making a toy fortress of it; and there is a tradition that a gun was put here, and sometimes fired. This mound was the "Lions' Den"; here he kept such animals as were most dangerous. In a field facing his sitting-room was a pond, where he kept for experiment his fishes, frogs, leeches, eels, and river-mussels; and it is said the pond was ornamented with the skulls of animals. The trees dotted about the grounds served him for his studies of the heat of living plants, their movements, and their power of repair. He kept fowls, ducks, geese, pigeons, rabbits, pigs, and made experiments on them; also opossums, hedgehogs, and rare animals—a jackal, a zebra, an ostrich, buffaloes, even leopards; also dormice, bats, snakes, and birds of prey. Sometimes the large beasts were troublesome, or worse:—

"The fiercer animals were those to which he was most partial, and he had several of the bull kind from different parts of the world. Among these was a beautiful small bull he had received from the Queen,

besides a prodigious variety of other beasts and birds supposed to be naturally hostile to each other." Long afterward, in 1886, just before the house was demolished, Dr. Merriman wrote an excellent account of it, with the assistance of Frank Buckland. It has been said that Hunter must have had early success in practice, to afford the purchase of land at Earl's Court in 1764; but it was in the country then, and so late as 1775 the house was rated at only £15 a year.

with which he used to wrestle in play, and entertain himself with its exertions in its own defence. In one of these contests the bull overpowered him, and got him down; and had not one of the servants accidentally come by, and frightened the animal away, this frolic would probably have cost him his life." . . .

"Two leopards, which were kept chained in an outhouse, had broken from their confinement, and got into the yard among some dogs, which they immediately attacked; the howling this produced alarmed the whole neighbourhood; Mr. Hunter ran into the yard to see what was the matter, and found one of them getting up the wall to make his escape, the other surrounded by the dogs; he immediately laid hold of them both, and carried them back to their den; but as soon as they were secured, and he had time to reflect upon the risk of his own situation, he was so much agitated that he was in danger of fainting."

All round the house was a covered area or cloister, about six feet below the level of the ground, useful for keeping small animals in cages, and for the rough work of anatomy. The way into this underground area was through a sunken passage, "very dark, and like an enlarged fox's earth," says Buckland, but large enough to admit a small cart or truck; and the stables were near the entrance of this passage. In them were stalls and kennels for all kinds of animals, tame or wild, that he kept for breeding, and for observation of their ways. In the conservatory were several hives of bees, and the wall-fruit in the garden was their sole property. There were also small dens close to the sunken passage : and a room with a large copper boiler for the making of skeletons.

Thus the house was beset on all sides by strange creatures, and witnessed a vast number of experiments on the living and dissections of the dead. Here he dissected the rorqual, seventeen feet long, mentioned in his "Observations on the Structure and Œconomy of Whales"; and here, in 1783, he made the skeleton of the Irish Giant :—

"Byrne, or O'Brien, the famous Irish giant, died in 1783. He had been in a declining state of health for some time previously, and Hunter, anxious to procure his skeleton, set his man Howison to keep watch on his movements, that he might be sure of securing his body at his death. Byrne learned this, and as he had a horror of being dissected, determined to take such precautions as should ensure his not falling into the hands of the doctors; he accordingly left strict orders that his body should be watched day and night, until a leaden coffin should be made, in which it was to be inclosed, and carried out to sea and sunk. Byrne died soon after, and, in compliance with his directions, the undertaker engaged some men to watch the body alternately. Howison soon learned this, found out the house where these men went to drink when off duty, and gave information to Hunter, who forthwith proceeded thither with the view of bribing them to allow the body to be carried off. He had an interview with one of the party at the alehouse, and began by offering him fifty pounds if he would allow the body to be kidnapped; the man agreed, provided his companions would consent, and went out to consult them. He returned shortly, saying that they must have a hundred pounds. Hunter consented to this, and thought the affair settled; but the men finding him so eager, soon came back with an increased demand, which was also agreed to; when further difficulties were found, and larger and larger demands made, until, it is said, they raised the price to five hundred pounds! The money was borrowed to pay them; and in the dead of night the body was removed in a hackney-coach, and after having been carried through several streets was transferred to Hunter's own carriage, and conveyed immediately to Earl's Court. Fearing lest a discovery should take place, Hunter did not choose to risk the delay which the ordinary mode of preparing a skeleton would require; accordingly, the body was cut to pieces, and the flesh separated by boiling; hence has arisen the brown colour of the bones, which in all other respects form a magnificent skeleton."[1]

Earl's Court House, thus set in the midst of wonders, was at first a plain square brick house; later,

[1] This is the account given by Ottley; a somewhat different version is given by Tom Taylor, on the authority of Clift.

it grew with the growth of Hunter's work there. His study was on the ground floor, looking over the garden toward the Lions' Den; the drawing-room, or morning-room, was also on the ground floor, opening into a conservatory. The best bedroom, on the first floor, was well decorated; "the panels were enriched with drawings representing Cupid and Psyche, finished in water-colours with true classic chastity by a near relation of Mrs. Hunter, a gentleman who had studied in the Italian school. Each compartment was bordered with a circular ornament, which concealed the nails by which it was attached to the wall, that the whole might be readily removed when the house was deserted for the winter season."[1]

We do not know how long Hunter had to wait for a fair amount of practice; and probably he did not care. Home says that his income, for the first eleven years of his practice, 1763–1774, never amounted to a thousand pounds; and that he always purchased some addition to his collection so soon as he had saved ten guineas in fees. But the years 1767 and 1768 brought with them some reward for him: first, as a man of science, then, as a surgeon.

In February, 1767, when he was now thirty-nine years old, he was elected a Fellow of the Royal Society, though he had not yet submitted to the

[1] Faulkner's "History of Kensington," 1820.

JOHN HUNTER

Society any of his work, except an appendix to a paper contributed, a few months before, by Mr. Ellis. It is strange that he should have received this honour ten years earlier than his brother : perhaps the publication of William Hunter's " Medical Commentaries " had given offence. This same year was marked by an event very different from his election to the Royal Society; he ruptured his Achilles tendon, and that by dancing :—

"I believe fracture of this tendon often happens when a person is fatigued and off his guard, as after dancing, &c., and after the muscles have acted spontaneously, as in the cramp; at least it happened to me after dancing, and after a violent fit of the cramp."

He refused to keep his bed, and got about on the third day, keeping his heel raised, his knee straight, and his leg bandaged; and in this fashion he afterward treated other cases like his own. He also made experiments on dogs, dividing the tendon subcutaneously, killing the dogs at different periods afterward, and examining the repaired tendons; thus foreshadowing Stromeyer's work in subcutaneous surgery.

On the 9th of December, 1768, on the resignation of Mr. Gataker, John Hunter was elected one of the surgeons to St. George's Hospital, by 114 votes, against his opponent Mr. Bayford, who received 42 votes. He was at this time forty years old, and he had before him twenty-five years yet to come. His election to St. George's Hospital was of infinite value to him. It has been said that a surgeon without a hospital is like a gardener without a garden. Now at last Hunter had got his garden, and he made it bear fruit a hundredfold. As his brother once said, " Were I to place a man of proper talents in the most direct road for becoming truly great in his profession, I would choose a good practical anatomist, and put him into a large hospital, to attend the sick, and dissect the dead."

One of the benefits that this appointment brought to John Hunter, was the right to have " house-pupils." They were bound to him for one or more years of teaching and of training ; they paid a fee of £100 per annum, and received from him not only education, but also board and lodging. Among his house-pupils— Mr. John Kingston, Mr. Guy of Chichester, Dr. Physick of Philadelphia, and others—one of the first of all, and the most famous of all, was Edward Jenner.

Soon after his appointment to St. George's Hospital he was made a member of the Corporation of Surgeons ; and in the years 1768–1771 he published his first book, moved house, and was married.[1]

His book, the first part of the "Treatise on the

---

[1] *From John Hunter to William Hunter.*

DEAR BROTHER,—To-morrow morning at eight o'clock and at St. James's Church I enter into the Holy State of Matrimony. As that is a ceremony which you are not particularly fond of, I will not make a point of having your company there. I propose going out of Town for a few days ; when I come to Town I shall call upon you. Married or not married, ever yours,

JOHN HUNTER.

JERMYN STREET, *Saturday Evening.*

Natural History of the Human Teeth," was published in May, 1771, two months before his marriage, and tradition says that he spent the profits of it on the expenses of the wedding. It was the only one of his writings that he sold to the booksellers; the rest were all published on his own account, or contained in the Transactions of different Societies; and it was translated into Dutch (Dordrecht, 1773) and Latin (Leipzig, 1775).

In 1768, when William Hunter moved house from Jermyn Street to Great Windmill Street, John Hunter took over the lease of the house in Jermyn Street, and moved into it from Golden Square.[1] It was a wise move, into a good house, in a fashionable part of London, near the hospital, and already known to everybody as a doctor's house. Henceforth the resident pupils would have no need to complain of their lodging; as for their board, Hunter might be somewhat forgetful. But he did not marry Miss Anne Home to get a housekeeper, for they had been engaged many years.

[1] The exact date of his moving house is not known; but we know that William Hunter's address was Jermyn Street in 1767, and Great Windmill Street in 1768.

IV

London 1772–1783.—Jermyn Street

"That the blood has life is an opinion I have stated for above thirty years, and have taught it for near twenty of that time in my lectures. . . . Organisation and life do not depend in the least upon each other: organisation may arise out of living parts, and produce action; but life never can arise out of, or depend on, organisation."

MRS. HUNTER was the elder daughter of Mr. Robert Boyne Home, surgeon to Burgoyne's Regiment of Light Horse, afterward of Greenlaw Castle, Berwickshire, and of Mary, daughter of Colonel Hutchinson. Even Jesse Foot found no fault in her. Ottley, fourteen years after her death, wrote: "She was an agreeable, clever, and handsome woman, a little of a *bas bleu*, and rather fond of gay society, a taste which occasionally interfered with her husband's more philosophic pursuits." But he must have said this for the sake of leading up to the well-known story about him:—

"On returning home late one evening, after a hard day's fag, Hunter unexpectedly found his drawing-room filled with musical professors, connoisseurs, and other idlers, whom Mrs. Hunter had assembled. He was greatly irritated, and walking straight into the room, addressed the astonished guests pretty much in the following strain : ' I knew nothing of this kick-up, and I ought to have been informed of it beforehand ; but as I am now returned home to study, I hope the present company will retire.' This intimation was of course speedily followed by an *exeunt omnes*."

Her name occurs many times in Hunter's letters to Jenner. "Mrs. Hunter and I were at Bath the other day ; we wished much we could have staid a day, to have waited on you. . . . Mrs. H. desires her compliments to you. . . . Anny sends her compliments, and thanks you for all favours. . . . Anny sends, with little John, their compliments." There are two portraits of her, many years apart, in Miss Baillie's possession ; they give evidence that in her old age she lost neither her wit nor her beauty ; and her husband's letter at the end of this chapter, and the reminiscences of her grand-niece at the end of Chap. VI., show that Ottley had a wrong idea of her. They also suggest that Hunter, between thirty and forty, conquered the roughness, ignorance, and isolation of his earlier life, or she would not have accepted him and waited for years for him.

She was twenty-nine when she married John Hunter (July, 1771), and he was forty-three. Their first child was born in June, 1772, and was named after his father. They had another son, James, who died in infancy ; a daughter, Mary Ann, who died young ; and another

LONDON, 1772-1783

daughter, Agnes. John went to Cambridge, and then into the army, and became a Colonel; he left no children. Agnes, who like her mother was beautiful and clever, married Captain Campbell, afterward Sir James Campbell; after his death she married Colonel Charleywood. She had no children by either marriage. At the time of their father's death, John had lately left Cambridge, and Agnes was between seventeen and eighteen years old.

When Hunter was at the zenith of his life, Mrs. Hunter was something more than the reflection of his light; she shone of herself; took her place high in society; was the friend of other clever and famous women—Madame D'Arblay, Mrs. Montagu. She wrote "My mother bids me bind my hair," which lives for ever in the setting that Haydn gave it,[1] and in her widowhood she published a volume of poems, and composed an epitaph, eleven years after Hunter's death, for a memorial tablet to him in St. Martin's-in-the-Fields :—

> Here rests in awful silence, cold and still,
>   One whom no common sparks of genius fired;
> Whose reach of thought Nature alone could fill,
>   Whose deep research the love of Truth inspired.
>
> Hunter! if years of toil and watchful care,
>   If the vast labours of a powerful mind
> To soothe the ills humanity must share,
>   Deserve the grateful plaudits of mankind—

---

[1] She also wrote the words for Haydn's "Creation." The rough draft of them, and a manuscript volume of her poems, are in the possession of Miss Baillie.

JOHN HUNTER

> Then be each human weakness buried here
> Envy would raise to dim a name so bright :
> Those specks which in the orb of day appear
> Take nothing from his warm and welcome light.

The colossal weight of Hunter's work, his overwhelming energy, then the slow ruin of his health, and the abiding fear of his death—these things ran up the price she paid for the honour of being his wife. In her widowhood, she became companion to two young ladies with fortunes, wards of Dr. Maxwell Garthshore, a kindly old gentleman, whom Hunter had been used to treat with good-natured contempt :—

"Dr. Garthshore was quite a physician of the old school, always well dressed and exceedingly polite, and a great favourite with the dowagers. He was intimate with John Hunter, who did not, however, treat him with much courtesy. One day the doctor, on entering the dissecting-room where Hunter was at work, began as usual, with great *empressement*, 'My d-e-a-r John Hunter.' 'My dear Tom Fool,' replied Hunter, looking up and imitating the tone and manner of the astonished doctor.'" (Ottley.)

"One morning, finding Mr. Hunter very busy in his Collection, Dr. Garthshore observed, 'Ah, John, you are always at work !' 'I am,' replied Mr. Hunter, 'and when I am dead, you will not soon meet with another John Hunter.'" (Adams.)

Turned for a time from John Hunter's wife to Dr. Garthshore's young ladies' companion, " in the receipt of a very handsome salary," and afterward living in a small house in Lower Grosvenor Street, first with her sister, finally alone,[1] Anne Hunter wore through twenty-seven years of widowhood, and died on January 7, 1821, seventy-nine years old. She kept her wit and her beauty to the end of her days; and the Hunterian Orator of 1821 paid to her memory this heavy compliment—that "she had sustained an honourable widowhood, estimable for talents of her own, and venerable as the relict of her illustrious husband."

In 1772, Mrs. Hunter's young brother, Everard Home, makes his first appearance on the scene; and for the part he played in and after Hunter's life, he must here introduce himself in his own words:—

"While Mr. Hunter was paying his addresses to my sister, Miss Home, I was a boy at Westminster School. During the holidays I came home, and Mr. Hunter, who was frequently there, always showed me particular kindness; he made my father an offer to bring me up to his profession, a proposal which I readily accepted. I was struck with the novelty and extent of his researches, had the highest respect and admiration for his talents, and was ambitious to tread the paths of science under so able a master. It is a tribute which I owe to his memory to declare that an intimate knowledge of him for one-and-twenty years

---

[1] Ottley appears to be wrong in saying she was companion to the young ladies till her death (see Mrs. Milligan's Reminiscences, chap. vi.).

JOHN HUNTER

(1772-1793) has increased my admiration of his uncommon exertions, and my respect for his abilities.

"After finishing my education at Westminster School as a king's scholar, and being elected off to Trinity College, Cambridge, I found that no advantages which I could have derived from a scholarship in the University could compensate for the time I must have given up in keeping my terms, to the disadvantage of my chirurgical education; I therefore thought it prudent to forego my claims upon the University as a king's scholar, and instead of going down to Cambridge, though elected, went immediately to Mr. Hunter.

"At this time his private practice and his professional character were advancing very fast, and his family had begun to increase, but still no small part of his time was devoted to his collection, which, as it daily became larger, was also attended with greater expence. The whole suite of the best rooms in his house was occupied by his preparations; and he dedicated his mornings from sunrise to eight o'clock (the hour for breakfast) entirely to his pursuits. To these he added such parts of the day as were not engaged in attending his patients."

There is something wrong with these cool sentences, written so soon after Hunter's death. For the present, young Home was set to his work, and learned the dissection and putting-up of specimens; and was told, he who had foregone his claims on a University, that his fingers were all thumbs, and that he would never have sense enough to tie down a bottle.

LONDON, 1772–1783

Next year, 1773, John Hunter suffered his first attack of angina pectoris:—

"I had the gout in my feet three springs successively, and missed it the fourth. In the fifth spring, one day at ten o'clock in the forenoon, I was attacked suddenly with a pain nearly about the pylorus; it was a pain peculiar to those parts, and became so violent that I tried every position to relieve myself, but could get no ease. I then took a teaspoonful of tincture of rhubarb, with thirty drops of laudanum, but still found no relief. As I was walking about the room, I cast my eyes on a looking-glass, and observed my countenance pale, my lips white, and I had the appearance of a dead man looking at himself. This alarmed me. I could feel no pulse in either arm. The pain still continuing, I began to think it very serious. I found myself at times not breathing; and being afraid of death soon taking place if I did not breathe, I produced a voluntary action of breathing, working my lungs by the power of my will. I continued in this state three-quarters of an hour, when the pain lessened, the pulse was felt, and involuntary breathing began to take place. During this state I took madeira, brandy, ginger, and other warm things; but I believe nothing did any good, as the return of health was very gradual. About two o'clock I was able to go about my business.

"Here, then, was a suspension of the most material involuntary actions, so much so that the involuntary action of breathing stopped, while sensation and all the voluntary actions were as strong as before.

JOHN HUNTER

"Quære, what would have been the consequence if I had not breathed? At the time, it struck me that I should have died; but that most probably would not have been the consequence, because, most probably, breathing is only necessary for the blood when it is circulating; but as there was no circulation going on, so no good could have arisen from breathing."

He remained free till 1776 from further attacks; and for several years after 1776 he had long intervals of freedom; but at last he came to be in pain every day. It will be best not to write out his case here, but to note its phases as they occurred: remembering that he was exposed by his life and temperament to the utmost heaviness of the disease.

This same year, 1773, he gave the first course of his lectures on the Principles of Surgery: thus he extended his work in the autumn, as it were in answer to the challenge Death had thrown him in the spring. Here is the advertisement of them:—

"*On Monday Evening, the 4th of October, at Seven o'Clock*, Mr. John Hunter will begin, at No. 28, in the Hay-market, a Course of Lectures on the Principles and Practice of SURGERY, in which will be introduced so much of the ANIMAL OECONOMY as may be necessary to illustrate the Principles of those Diseases which are the Object of Surgery. This course will be continued on Mondays, Wednesdays, and Fridays, through the whole Winter, at the Hour above mentioned. Proposals may be seen, and Tickets will be delivered, in Jermyn-Street. No Person will be admitted to the first Lecture without a Ticket for the Course."

The labour of preparing and delivering these magnificent lectures was very heavy; there was nothing like them in London, for their comprehension of the whole circle of the sciences round surgery. The *European Magazine* of 1782 says, "This very celebrated Course consists of near an hundred Lectures. It begins in the month of October, and continues till April, and is given every other evening, from seven to eight o'clock, the honorarium being four guineas. Thus the lectures cost his hearers tenpence apiece for each lecture. What did they cost Hunter? We have Home, Abernethy, and Cline to answer this question:—

"Giving lectures was always particularly unpleasant to him: so that the desire of submitting his opinions to the world, and learning their general estimation, was scarcely sufficient to overcome his natural dislike to speaking in public. He never gave the first lecture of his course without taking thirty drops of laudanum to take off the effects of his uneasiness. He was so diffident of himself that he trusted nothing to memory, and made me draw up a short abstract of each lecture, which he read on the following evening as a recapitulation, to connect the subject in the minds of the students." (Home.)

"I was acquainted with Mr. Hunter at a period of his life when he must have greatly interested any one who duly appreciated the results of his talents and labours, or who had any sympathy for the highly susceptible mind of genius, rendered still more so by excess of exertion, and the perturbed feelings incident to bodily disease. He seemed to me conscious of his own desert, of the insufficiency and uncertainty of his acquirements, and of his own inability readily to communicate what he knew and thought. He felt irritated by the opposition he had met with . . . 'I know, I know,' said he, 'I am but a pigmy in knowledge, yet I feel as a giant, when compared with these men.'" (Abernethy.)

"When only twenty-four years of age, I had the happiness of hearing the first course of lectures which John Hunter delivered. I had been at that time for some years in the profession, and was tolerably well acquainted with the opinions held by the surgeons most distinguished for their talent then residing in the metropolis; but having heard Mr. Hunter's lectures on the subject of disease, I found him so far superior to anything I had conceived or heard before, that there seemed no comparison between the great mind of the man who delivered them, and all the individuals, whether ancient or modern, who had gone before him." (Cline.)

Tenpence apiece for lectures thus wrung out of Hunter's life was not excessive; yet Jesse Foot called at Jermyn Street, asked for a syllabus, found he could get nothing for nothing, and declined paying anything;

LONDON, 1772-1783

and wrote, so soon as Hunter was dead, "Instead of lecturing at the hospital, free of expense to its pupils, as was done by Pott, and of openly imparting his system to those who were desirous of increasing the stock of surgical knowledge, Mr. Hunter could by lecturing at home[1] shut out every one capable of comparing his dogmas with established doctrines, infuse without contradiction his principles into the minds of his pupils, and take their money into the bargain."

The first two courses of lectures were given, free of all payment, to the pupils of St. George's Hospital and a few of Hunter's friends. The dissecting-room at Jermyn Street was open to those who attended the lectures : preparations from the museum were shown at each lecture, and at the end of it questions were asked and answered. The lectures were not a compulsory part of medical education ; at some of the courses he had fifty men listening to him ; later, in 1786, he had only twelve. The immeasurable extent of his thoughts over-strained the attention of these young men. The Principles of Surgery were not practice, but embryology, physiology, and animal chemistry ; the properties of matter, the vital principle, the life of the blood. He himself was not at ease : he read his manuscript, keeping his eyes upon it, and having recourse to rough notes to correct the text. He loved

[1] In 1779, the lectures were given at 28, Haymarket ; in 1783, at Hunter's house in Castle Street.

to sacrifice the outward form of his teaching, that he might be for ever improving the substance of it :—

"To Astley Cooper, who asked with surprise whether he had not, the year before, stated an opinion on some point directly at variance with one he had just put forth, he replied 'Very likely 1 did : I hope I grow wiser every year,' and to the same purport he answered another of his pupils, who asked whether he had not written so-and-so, 'Never ask me what I have said, or what I have written ; but if you will ask me what my present opinions are, I will tell you.' Occasionally too he would say to any of the pupils whom he saw taking notes, 'You had better not write down that observation, for very likely I shall think differently next year' : and on one occasion, after lecturing for a considerable time, he stopped short, raised his spectacles, and said, 'Gentlemen, I think you had better omit what I have been saying : the fact is, I had an idea when I wrote down this, but I have lost the train of thought connected with it, and I cannot now recall it.' This was a difficulty he not unfrequently experienced." (Ottley.)

Certain phrases, which were no more than metaphors, he overburdened with meaning, if by any method he could describe life : such were sympathy, affinity, the irritation of imperfection, the stimulus of death, the blood's consciousness of its being a useful part of the body, the consent of the fluids with the solids, the stimulus of nature, the stimulus of necessity for coagulation of the blood. A curious instance of this abuse of words occurs in his account of the absorption of diseased or superfluous tissues within the body :—

"The remote cause of absorption of whole and living parts implies the existence of two conditions, the first of which is a consciousness, in the parts to be absorbed, of the unfitness or impossibility of remaining under such circumstances, whatever they may be, and therefore they become ready for removal, and submit to it with ease. The second is a consciousness, of the absorbents, of such a state of the parts. Both these concurring, they have nothing to do but to fall to the work. Now the part that is to be absorbed is alive, it must feel its own inefficacy and admit of absorption. The vessels must have the stimulus of imperfection of this part, as if they were sensible that this part were unfit; and therefore take it up. There must be a sensation in both parts. When the part to be absorbed is a dead part, then the whole disposition is in the absorbents."

But his genius made him practical in the things of practice. It was the same John Hunter who said to Cline, "I love to think," who wrote to Jenner, "But why think? Why not try the experiment?" When he came to lecture on this or that disease or injury, the diagnosis and treatment of it, he was plain-spoken, full of hard common sense, a rough critic, fond of a good anecdote. Sometimes he quoted cases from his private practice: "This kind of fracture happened to the

Archbishop of Canterbury. . . . When the Duke of Queensberry broke his tendo Achillis. . . . Lord Cavendish's father always felt pain in the left arm from a stone in the bladder. . . . General Murray, to whom I have often expressed a wish to peep into his chest, was twice wounded in this way." Sometimes he used phrases more strong than elegant; but he never told coarse stories. He confessed repeatedly his own ignorance, and sometimes his own mistakes; he was ready to find fault with other men, especially with the physicians. Thus he says of phthisis, "The physicians here keep their patients as long as they can, and then send them away to Bristol and other places to die;" and of tetanus, "I attended another case, with Sir N. Thomas. Assafœtida and opium were given without effect; these were left off, and bark given in large quantities. Dr. Warren being called in, advised among other things a bath prepared of milk and water. After this he seemed better, but died soon after. I discovered to my amazement the different methods of different physicians. Sir N. Thomas had read much, and knew all the antispasmodics from the days of Hippocrates downwards. Dr. Warren, having just cured his son of locked jaw, implicitly followed the same practice in this case, being unable to alter his rules of practice in the smallest degree as occasion might require." Certainly Hunter was not thus straitened in his treatment of a case of carbuncle :—

"As neither bark nor calomel nor opium had been

of any use, I said to Dr. David Pitcairn, 'Now do not let us permit this patient to be lost, whilst we are only using such means as experience shows to be of little or no effect; for, David, this is a case more belonging to my province than yours, and I, being an older man, have seen more of them than you have, and can tell you what perhaps you did not know, that we have no powers in this case that are known.' Now David is a truly sensible man, and not governed by form; he therefore agreed, but wanted to know where we were to begin. 'Why, with the first letter of the alphabet, and go through the catalogue of the materia medica; so as we do not stop too long on the letter B (bark) as is generally done.'"

After this treatment, the patient recovered. Or we may take, as one more illustration of Hunter's unrivalled straightforwardness of words, the following paragraph :—

"Arsenic is a remedy which enters into the empirical nostrums which are in vogue for curing cancer; and among which Plunkett's holds the highest rank. But this is no new discovery: for Sennertus, who lived the Lord knows how long ago, mentions a Roderiguez and Flusius, who obtained considerable fame and fortune by such a composition. I was desired to meet Mr. Plunkett, to decide on the propriety of using his medicines in a particular case: I have no objection to meet anybody: it was the young one; the old one is dead, and might have died himself of a cancer for aught I know. I asked him what he intended to do with his medicine. He said, 'To cure the patient.' 'Let me know what you mean by that; do you mean to alter the diseased state of the parts? or do you mean by your medicine to remove the parts diseased?' 'I mean to destroy them,' he replied. 'Well, then, that is nothing more than I or any other surgeon can do, with less pain to the patient.' Poor Woollett, the engraver, died under one of these cancer-curers; he was under my care when this person took him in hand —he had been a life-guardsman, I think, and had got a never-failing receipt. I continued to call on Woollett as a friend, and received great accounts of the good effects; upon hearing which, I said if the man would give me leave to watch regularly and see myself the good effects, I would exert all my power to make him the richest man in the kingdom. But he would have nothing to do with me, and tortured poor Woollett for some time, till at length he died."

Tenpence apiece for a hundred lectures such as these! Happy pupils—privileged for four guineas to sit at Hunter's feet for six months! From their notes, copies of the lectures were made, which were passed from hand to hand. There are several such manuscripts in the possession of the Royal College of Surgeons. Palmer's edition of the lectures (1835) was printed from shorthand notes, taken in 1786–87 by Mr. Nathaniel Rumsey, of Chesham; and from copies belonging to Sir Benjamin Brodie and others.

LONDON, 1772–1783

In 1775, Hunter first earned above a thousand pounds by one year's practice. But he never dropped one burden because he had shouldered another; in spite of the lectures, the increase of his private practice, and his work at the hospital, he was engaged on innumerable dissections, observations, and experiments. In the years 1772–1776, he contributed seven papers to the Philosophical Transactions of the Royal Society, five of them in comparative anatomy or physiology, one in pathology, and one only, out of the seven, concerned with treatment. Moreover, he was for ever adding to the preparations in his museum; "his first floor, and back apartments, were filling apace, insomuch that he was not able to find room for the *Camela Perda*, given him by Lady S——, the tallest animal known, and which browses upon the branches of trees; he therefore, that it might be in sight, cut off its legs, and fixed it in the passage."

From 1772 onward, he made frequent use of Earl's Court House, sleeping there during the autumn months, coming into the town in the morning, returning to dinner. Mrs. Hunter must choose between the house in Jermyn Street, with her rooms invaded by anatomical preparations, and the villa at Earl's Court, with its grounds full of strange or hostile animals. He could do with only five hours of sleep; and of his daily life for many years Ottley gives this account:—

"He commenced his labours in the dissecting-room

generally before six in the morning, and remained there till nine, when he breakfasted. After breakfast, he saw patients at his own house until twelve, when he made it a point to set forth on his rounds, even though persons might be in waiting for the purpose of seeing him. . . . He dined at four, then the fashionable hour, and gave strict orders that dinner should be ready punctually whether he was at home or not. He was a very moderate eater, and set little value on the indulgence of the palate. During many of the latter years of his life, he drank no wine, and therefore seldom remained long at table after dinner, except when he had company. After dinner he was accustomed to sleep for about an hour, and his evenings were spent either in preparing or delivering lectures, in dictating to an amanuensis the records of particular cases, of which he kept a regular entry, or in a similar manner committing to paper the substance of any work on which he chanced to be engaged. When employed in the latter way, Mr. Bell[1] and he used to retire to the study, the former carrying with him from the museum such preparations as related to the subject on which Hunter was engaged; these were placed on the table before him, and at the other end sat Mr. Bell, writing from Hunter's dictation. The manuscript was then looked over, and the grammatical blunders—for Bell was an uneducated man—

[1] William Bell, anatomist and artist, came to Hunter in 1775, and lived in the house for fourteen years.

corrected by Hunter. At twelve, the family went to bed, and the butler, before retiring to rest, used to bring in a fresh argand lamp, by the light of which Hunter continued his labours until one or two in the morning, or even later in winter. Thus he left only about four hours for sleep, which with the hour after dinner was all the time that he devoted to the refreshment of his body. He had no home amusements, no cards, for the relaxation of his mind; and the only indulgence of this kind he enjoyed consisted in an evening's ramble amongst the various denizens of earth and air which he had congregated at Earl's Court."

In January, 1776, he was appointed Surgeon Extraordinary to the King; his brother had been twelve years already a member of the Household. The same year, he gave the first of his Croonian Lectures before the Royal Society, on Muscular Motion. The lectures, six in all, were read during the years 1776–1782; and included his observations on the movements of plants. "These lectures were not published in the Philosophical Transactions; for they were withdrawn as soon as read, not being considered by the author as complete dissertations, but rather as materials for some future publication." (Home.)

Early in 1777, he had a strange illness, closely related to angina; in its general features, and resemblance to the night-terrors of children, it might be called epileptiform. "He had no sooner lain down than he felt as if suspended in the air, and soon after the room appeared to go round; the quickness of this motion seemed to increase, and at last became very rapid. . . . If he but moved his head half round, it appeared to be moving to some distance with great velocity; the idea he had of his own size was that of being only two feet long, and when he drew up his foot, or pushed it down, it appeared to him to be moving a vast way. His sensations became extremely acute or heightened; he could not bear the least light, he kept his eyelids closed, his hearing was also painfully acute. . . . At the end of ten days, all his ideas of his present state became more natural, the strange deception concerning his own size was in part corrected, and the idea of suspension in the air became less; but for some time after, the fire appeared of a deep purple red. When he got so well as to be able to stand without being giddy, he was unable to walk without support, for his own feelings did not give him information respecting his centre of gravity, so that he was unable to balance his body." (Home.)

After this illness, he went to Bath, and drank the waters there. But before he left town, he made arrangements for a catalogue of his museum, that it might be sold at a fair price if he should die; he had nothing else to leave his family. Everard Home and Bell were set to write descriptions of the preparations; but some of them Hunter himself must describe; and anxiety about the catalogue, and inability to live without work, brought him back to London in less than three months, not yet restored to his former health.

Back in Jermyn Street, he took up everything again, and added to his other occupations a further series of experiments on the heat of animals and vegetables, which were published in the Philosophical Transactions of the Royal Society.

In 1778, he published the second part of his Treatise on the Natural History of the Human Teeth ; on the diseases of the teeth and of the adjacent parts, and their treatment. This same year, Everard Home left him, and he had only Mr. Bell to help him in all the work of the lectures and the museum :—

"I had now lived six years with Mr. Hunter, and had completed my education : his expenses had always exceeded his income. I had therefore no emolument to expect from remaining in his house, which made it necessary for me to take up some line for my own support ; and Admiral Keppel's action with the French fleet was the means of procuring me a very eligible situation. The newly finished naval hospital at Plymouth received the whole of the wounded men from Admiral Keppel's fleet, and Dr. Farquarson, the first commissioner of sick and hurt, at the request of Mr. Adair, the present surgeon-general to the garrison of Gibraltar, gave me the appointment of assistant-surgeon, with apartments to reside at the hospital. . . . In this situation many opportunities occurred to me of adding to Mr.

Hunter's collection; the sea furnishing curious fish and other marine productions; and the hospital practice, preparations of morbid parts."

When Home went off to his eligible situation at Plymouth, John Hunter was fifty years old; Surgeon Extraordinary to the King, Surgeon to St. George's Hospital, and a Fellow of the Royal Society; having a large practice, and a name known everywhere. Yet he never saved money; he was for ever adding to his museum, till he had spent no less than £70,000 on it, and he died scarce able to pay his debts. To have an idea of his absolute devotion of himself to scientific work, we must realise that he lavished on science the income that he made at the risk of his life by the hard work of practice, and even in ill-health and under the shadow of death never rested from his incessant task of collection, dissection, observation, and experiment. The letters to Jenner show the marvellous restlessness of these years from 1779 to 1783, full of science and of practice, added or rather multiplied together. Honours came to him from abroad, from Gothenburg and Paris. The house in Jermyn Street could now no longer hold his collection, and he must move elsewhere, even at the cost of a bad bargain. Over everything hung the clouds of want of money, illhealth, and estrangement from his brother.

William Hunter died on Sunday, March 30, 1783. In his will, he did not so much as name John Hunter; he left Long Calderwood away from him to

Matthew Baillie; he left nothing to John, entrusted nothing to his care. Adams tells the story to the end:—

"Whatever may have been the coldness of this dying philosopher, John felt the parting scene most severely. This was remarked by us all, as he entered the lecture room, and most when a particular circumstance obliged him to mention his brother's death.

" The spring was advancing, and his course was finished. On this occasion I shall transcribe from my notes, taken at the time, the conclusion of his peroration, which was given *extempore*.

" Having finished his course, Mr. Hunter affectionately addressed his pupils in the usual form, expressing his gratitude for the tribute they had paid his abilities in attending his course during the winter; assuring them that he should ever be happy to see or hear from them, and to assist them with his advice—with a fee, if his patient's circumstances should admit, if not, as readily without, begging that the latter might never prevent their applying to him. It was, at present, his intention to continue lecturing in the same way as he had hitherto done. Some persons had suggested to him that he should lecture on anatomy; but he did not scruple to say that he thought himself superior to describing the origin and insertion of muscles, and the course of blood-vessels. He assumed the privilege of teaching the *action* of parts whose *situation* common application might easily demonstrate. Mere human anatomy was too small a scale for him to move in;

he had never been contented with it, and he trusted he had done as much in *comparative* anatomy, as it is called, as any one before him. Should his life and health permit, it was his wish at some period to undertake physiological lectures, not on the human alone, but on animals at large. He had neither sufficiently arranged his ideas, nor made up his opinion on some things, to begin for years.

"Some other remarks followed, on his prospects and on the new house he was preparing, which prevented his exhibiting his museum, as was his custom at the end of each course.

"Here Mr. Hunter seemed to finish, yet to have more to say; at length, endeavouring to appear as if he had just recollected something, he began : 'Ho, gentlemen, one thing more, I need not remind you of —you all know the loss anatomy has lately sustained!' He was obliged to pause, and turn his face from his hearers. At length, recovering himself, he proceeded, 'Though it would be unfair to compare Mr. Cruikshank with Dr. Hunter, yet much allowance should be made for Mr. Cruikshank, in being obliged at present to give lectures for which he could have made no preparation, as he could not expect that he should have occasion to give them; I have therefore only to beg you will make this allowance for him, and to acquaint you that the lectures will be continued as usual.'

"This, and a few words more, were not spoken

without great emotion, nor with dry eyes. The scene was so truly pathetic, that a general sympathy pervaded the whole class; and every one, though all had been preparing to leave the place, stood or sat motionless and silent for some minutes."

From John Hunter to the Rev. James Baillie, his brother-in-law, on his appointment to the Professorship of Divinity at Glasgow, 1775.

DEAR SIR,—I thank you for your very kind and obliging Letter. I also congratulate you upon your preferment. Altho you modestly say it was upon your family's account that you received it, yet it is what you should not have refused upon your own. There is hardly any character so low, or so high, but what will receive dignity from Title, and when it is given as a reward for merit, it gives the graces to it.

As to myself, with respect to my family, I can only yet say, that I am happy in a wife, but my children are too young to form any judgment of. They consist of a stout red-headed Boy, called Jock, three years and some months old, and a weakly girl call'd Mary-Ann, near two. We lost a fine boy call'd Jemmy who would have been now about twelve months; and Anny is near her time of a fourth.

I am not anxious about my children but in their doing well in this world. I would rather make them feel one moral virtue, than read Librarys of all the dead and living languages. You know I am no *Scholara*, therefore do not feel the beauty of Language, when I do not see the use of it; but if that should be the line which I meant they should follow, I should think myself happy in having such a Brother, and in such a situation. As to myself, I am pursuing business, and pursuing my studies. As to my business, it is very nearly what I want, because it very nearly gets me what I want; beyon which I have no ambition. As to my studies, I am following my business as a student, pursuing my comparative anatomy; for two or three months in the year, pretty much in the country making experiments upon animals and vegetables, and it appears to be Anny's enjoyment, in seeing me pleasing myself; while all these concurring circumstances go on, I must continue to be one of the happyst men living. I am sorry my sister is not well, health is one of the first principles in life, but I hope the complaint is such as not to be very uneasie to her, at least they are such as are not dangerous.

Anny joins with me in our best wishes to you and Dolly, and also to our young Nephew and nieces; and may hope to see the young man in London soon.

I am Dear Sir
Your most affectionate Brother
JOHN HUNTER.

Nov. 23rd, 1775.

V

Hunter and Jenner

"I don't know any one I would as soon write to as you. I do not know anybody I am so much obliged to."

SIXTEEN years ago Prof. S. D. Gross, of Philadelphia, himself one of the "Masters of Medicine," published a short Life of Hunter, with some account of the more famous of his pupils. Among them were Astley Cooper, Abernethy, Physick, Thomson, Cline—who had the spirit of Hunter, "et quasi cursores vitai lampada tradunt." One of the first of these pupils was Edward Jenner, who became a resident pupil so early as 1770, when he was but twenty-one years old; and lived two years in Hunter's house. He came to be of that inner circle of friends who called Hunter "the dear man"; and when he settled in practice at Berkeley in Gloucestershire, the friendship made in London was maintained and strengthened by the interchange of letters between the two men on every subject at which they could work together. He was the faithful image of Hunter, his second self down in Gloucestershire; and in 1777, when Hunter visited Bath after his second attack of angina, Jenner had already guessed the nature of his disease, but had said nothing to him about it, only writing what he thought of him to Dr. Heberden, who had charge of Hunter's case.

The letters to Jenner were first published in 1835, in Ottley's "Life of Hunter."[1] They make no mention of vaccination; the discovery was not firmly and finally established in Hunter's lifetime. They are most of them undated: and Ottley has corrected their spelling. I add only a few words of preface here and there, and omit only such details of anatomy, surgery, and experimental work, as must be read in their relation to the rest of Hunter's observations.

---

1 (? 1772).

DEAR JENNER,—I received yours, and was extremely happy to hear of your success in business;

---

[1] "Dr. Jenner set a great value upon these letters. They were carefully preserved in a cover, which was inscribed in his own handwriting, 'Letters from Mr. Hunter to E. Jenner'; an honour which he was not always in the habit of conferring on more dignified communications. . . . It was a truly interesting thing to hear Dr. Jenner, in the evening of his days, descanting with all the fervour of youthful friendship and attachment on the commanding and engaging peculiarities of Mr. Hunter's mind. He generally called him 'the dear man,' and when he described the honesty and warmth of his heart, and his never-ceasing energy in the pursuit of knowledge, it was impossible not to be animated by the recital." (Baron's "Life of Jenner.")

I hope it will continue. I am obliged to you for thinking of me, especially in my natural history. I shall be glad of your observations on the cuckoo, and upon the breeding of toads; be as particular as you possibly can. If you can pick me up anything that is curious and prepare it for me, either in the fish or flesh way, do it. Pictures have been very cheap, but the season is now over. There will be but one sale, viz., Fordyce's; but I believe all his pictures are exquisite, and will go beyond you or me. Since you wrote to me I purchased a small landscape of Barrett's, of cattle and herd; I gave five pounds seven shillings and sixpence; it is one of his eight-guinea pictures. You shall have it or not, as you please. I have one of the same size, that I bought of him some time ago.

I saw the young lady, your patient; I do not know well what can be done. . . . Let me hear from you soon.

Ever yours,
JOHN HUNTER.

II (? 1773).

DEAR JENNER,—I received yours, as also the cuckoo's stomach: I should like to have a few more, for they do not all show the same thing. If possible, I wish you could remove the cuckoo's egg into another bird's nest, and tame the young one, to see what note it has. There is employment for you, young man! If you collect eggs, you should also collect the nests, and I do not care how many you send. I wanted a crow's nest, as also a magpie's, in the branches of the trees where they are built, but I am afraid it is now too late.

This evening, looking into my book of patients to scratch out the name of one who had paid me, and whose name began with M, I saw a Mr. Matthews or Berkeley, recommended by you. He did not pay me. I forget whether he was recommended by you as a friend to serve him or me; if it was to serve him, I scratch him out of my book. Do you keep an account of your observations on the cuckoo, or must I refer to your letters? I want a nest with the eggs in it; also one with a young cuckoo; also an old cuckoo. I hear you saying, there is no end of your wants.

Ever yours,
JOHN HUNTER.

Jenner did keep an account of his observations on the cuckoo, and many years afterward communicated them to the Royal Society. The next two letters were written in 1775; they refer to Hunter's plan of founding a school of natural history in London, with Jenner to help him; but the scheme was not carried out.

HUNTER AND JENNER

III.

DEAR JENNER,—I have received many things from you, and will thank you in the lump; but while I thank you, I have a great scheme to communicate to you, and I want you to take part in it; but remember, it is as yet a most profound secret. My scheme is to teach natural history, in which will be included anatomy, both human and comparative. The labour of it is too much for one man, therefore I must have some one to assist; but who that person shall be is the difficulty. When running over a variety of people, you have come into my mind among the rest. Now, if it is a scheme you would like, and a possibility of your leaving the country,— at the same time, able and willing to lay down one thousand guineas—I will send you the whole proposals; but if you cannot leave the country on any terms, then it is unnecessary to go any further; and all I have to beg is to keep it a secret. I would not have you mention it to Ludlow, &c. I proposed it to L—— before he left London, but his father objected, I believe, to the money. I know the scheme will be to your taste. Before you ask any of your friends, consult with yourself, and ask, Can I go to London, and can I give one thousand guineas for any chance that may be worth it? Let me hear from you very soon.

Yours,

LONDON, *May* 24*th.*   JOHN HUNTER.

JOHN HUNTER

IV.

August 2nd.

Dear Jenner,—I received yours in answer to mine, which I should have answered. I own I suspected it would not do; yet as I did intend such a scheme, I was inclinable to give you the offer.

I thank you for your experiment on the hedgehog; but why do you ask me a question by the way of solving it? I think your solution is just; but why think? why not try the experiment? Repeat all the experiments upon a hedgehog as soon as you receive this, and they will give you the solution . . . and let me know the result of the whole.

Ever yours,
J. Hunter.

The next six letters were probably written between the end of 1775 and the spring of 1777; about the time of Hunter's earlier work on the vital heat of vegetables and animals.

V.

Dear Jenner,—I don't know any one I would as soon write to as you. I do not know anybody I am so much obliged to. I thank you for a fish, but I should thank you more if you had let me know who it comes from.

I beg for the future you will always write when

you send me anything. Somebody sent me a cheese, with a fish upon it; perhaps it was you; you know I hate to be puzzled. Also let me know what things you have sent me lately. I have not received the cuckoo's nest yet. Now for your patient. I believe the best thing you can do is to do little. I would not touch the fungus with an escharotic, for fear the brain should be near: I would also use but very slight compression, as the fungus will be a bandage to the brain; and as to the fungus itself you have nothing to fear, for wherever the parts underneath are sound, the fungus will subside of itself. Keep your patient rather low, and quiet. Let me know how he goes on, and anything else you can.

Ever yours,
J. H.

VI.

Jan. 10*th*.

DEAR JENNER,—You must think me very fond of fish when you send me cheese as much fishified as possible; however, it is an excellent cheese, and every country has laid claim to its birth. I have but one order to send you, which is, to send everything you can get, either animal, vegetable, or mineral, and the compound of the two, either animal or vegetable mineralised.

I would have you do nothing with the boy but

dress him superficially; these funguses will die, and be damned to them, and drop off.

Have you large trees, of different kinds, that you can make free with? If you have, I will put you upon a set of experiments with regard to the heat of vegetables.

Have you any eaves, where bats go to at night? If you have, I will put you upon a set of experiments concerning the heat of them at different seasons. I should have been extremely happy to have had the honour of a visit from Lord Berkeley.

Ever yours,
JOHN HUNTER.

Anny sends her compliments, and thanks you for all favours. Write down the case.

VII.

Jan. 22*nd*.

DEAR JENNER,—I did not understand that the funguses which you described were brain; and I should still very much doubt that they are brain, for their keeping into one substance would make me inclinable to believe that it is a new substance: but let it be what it will, I would advise you not to meddle with it: if it is brain, let it drop off; if it is fungus, let it either drop or waste off: therefore be quiet, and think yourself well off that the boy is not dead. You do not mention a word about bats. I have no particular experiments at present about

HUNTER AND JENNER

fixed air; it is such a wide field that a man may make a thousand experiments before he determines anything. Have you got the bones yet of a large porpoise? I wish you had. Is ever the salmon spawn seen after she has parted with it? If it is so, I would you could get me some; I want to examine the spawn of fish in the progress of the formation of the young one.

I am, dear Jenner,
Your most obedient Servant,
JOHN HUNTER.

VIII.

DEAR JENNER,—I received the box; also your letter. I am very much obliged to you for your kind attention to me, and how to reward you I do not know. Let that be as it will, I must still give you commissions. If you can get me easily salmon spawn, I should like to have it, and out of different places, as it will be of different ages. It should be put into bottles immediately, with spirits. The spirits should be proof, and there should be rather more spirit than spawn. I will also take any specimens of fossils you may send me, or indeed anything else. Did I send you any of my publications in the Philosophical Transactions? If I have not, let me know. I want to put you upon some experiments this winter. What do you think of examining eels? Their sexes have not yet been found out, nor their mode of propagation; it is a thing of consequence in natural history. I began it, but could not get eels immediately from the river, and to get them of fishmongers, who buy them in custom, does not do. My intention was to examine several pretty large eels on the first and fifteenth of every month. If the eels are plenty with you, and if you like the proposal, let me know, and I will give you full instructions how to proceed. Also, next spring, I would have you make the experiments on the growth of vegetables; and if you have no objection, I will set you upon a set of experiments upon the heat of vegetables in the winter. If, in any of these pursuits, you discover any principle worthy of the public, I will give it to the Royal Society for you. I must pick you up a picture this winter. I saw Mrs. Black[1] at Mr. Drummond's; I suspect Mr. Black is dead, but I durst not enquire. Cannot you get me a large porpoise for love or money? What is the bird you sent me? also the young animals, which I imagine to be guinea-pigs.

Ever yours,
JOHN HUNTER.

IX.

DEAR JENNER,—I received your salmon, and very fresh, and just examined enough to want another, but will wait till another season. If I was to have

---

[1] Mrs. Black was Jenner's elder sister, Mary, wife of the Rev. G. C. Black, of Norwood.

another, it should be one that had just spawned; I will take a cock salmon when you please. If you catch any bats, let me have some of them; and those you try yourself, observe the heat; observe the fluidity of the blood. . . . Do all this in a cold place. Extraneous fossils are all vegetable and animal substances found in a fossil state. See if you can catch the number of pulsations and breathing in a bat without torture. If the frost is hard, see what vegetables freeze: bore holes in large trees, and see whether the sap runs out, which will show it is not frozen. I am afraid you have not a proper thermometer: I will send you one.[1]

Your very much obliged Servant,
J. Hunter.

I have not seen Dr. H., but I dare say he will be glad to have the cases.

X.

Dear Jenner,—I can never be offended with you. The reason for not sending the thermometer was I entirely forgot it, but it shall be sent next week. I shall be glad to present your paper if you mean to give it to the public. The large porpoise I would have coarsely stripped, and the bones put into a cask and sent; the young one, if not too large, put into spirits, to be able to inject it. . . . Did I write to

[1] For his observations on animal heat, Hunter had made for himself a small thermometer, like the clinical thermometers of the present day.

you some time ago about cuckoos? I have forgot: if I did not, I must give you a long order.

    I am, dear Jenner,
       Ever yours,
         J. HUNTER.

Friday night.

I was at my club last night, and not coming home till twelve is the reason I did not write.

XI.

DEAR JENNER,—I have received your fish, as also your letter; for both I thank you. It came quite fresh, and it is under dissection and drawing. . . . I will leave it to you what is to be done at present with the bones; either send them as they are, or steep them in water. . . . I have got the thermometer, but let me know to whose care I am to send it. You did not in your last tell me if I wrote to you about the cuckoo.

       Ever yours,
         J. HUNTER.

The next three letters were written soon after Hunter's illness in 1777.

XII.

DEAR JENNER,—I have before me two letters of yours, which I should have answered much sooner. Your friend Dr. Hicks I have not seen. I was not at home when he called, and I have not had time to wait on him, as he lived entirely out of my walk. I should have been glad to have seen him, but I suppose he stood upon ceremony. I received the fossils, and should be glad of any that you can get. If any bones of animals are found, be sure and get them for me. I should be glad to have some of the salmon-fry. I had the pleasure of seeing your brother, but only for a time. I received the bird; I am not acquainted with it: send me some more if you can get them readily. I sent with Mr. Jenner the thermometer; if you do not understand it, let me know.

Not two hours after I saw your brother I was taken ill with a swimming in my head, and could not raise it off the pillow for ten days: it is not yet perfectly recovered. Have you begun the eels? No porpoises. No salmon spawn before it has hatched. You see I am very greedy. Be sure to keep an account of all outgoings.

My compliments to Mrs. Black and your brother, and let me hear from you.

Ever yours,
J. HUNTER.

LONDON, *May* 11, 1777.

XIII.

DEAR JENNER,—Excuse me for not answering your letters as soon as you could wish. Send me all the fossils you find. What I meant by bones was all the bones that are found any depth below the surface of the earth : many are found in stones, &c. I suppose those skeletons are not complete, but send me some of them ; and if any history can be given, send it also. The thermometer is a very useful one when understood. You will observe the scratch upon the glass stalk, perhaps about two inches from the globe, which is the freezing point ; put 0, or nought, which is upon the ivory scale, two degrees below the scratch, then 0 becomes the thirtieth degree, and the scratch, being two degrees above it, stands at the freezing point ; then, from that count upwards ; or if the cold is below 30°, then put 1 or 2 at the scratch, and count down ; every No. is ten degrees. What the devil becomes of your eels in the winter ? but try them in summer, and see what you can make of them.

I do not remember Dr. Fordyce ever supposing a polypus vascular. I should rather believe that he supposed the contrary ; you know that it comes near my idea that the blood is the bond of union everywhere. But I should very much suspect that a polypus formed after death is not of that kind. I am pretty certain that I have injected them in arteries after amputation. I have a preparation which shows it, and which supports my theory.

Yours,
J. Hunter.

London, *July* 6, 1777.

HUNTER AND JENNER

XIV.

Aug. 6, 1777.

DEAR JENNER,—I just now found your last letter. I think I answered it, but am not sure; if I did not, let me know. Is there any judging whose these human bones are? Let us have some of them, especially skulls, as complete as possible, with the lower jaw, &c. I am very well, but for all that I set out, in a few days, for Bath.

Ever yours,

J. HUNTER.

The next letter was written from Bath, whither Hunter had gone to recover his strength, and to be near his friend.

XV.

DEAR JENNER,—Till yesterday we did not know from whom the hare came; but the cook found it out. We thank you: it was a very fine one. By your not taking any notice of my letter, I do suppose you did not receive it. Near three weeks ago I wrote to you to meet us at the Hotwells, Bristol. Some days after the date of my letter we went to the appointed place, by ten o'clock in the morning; but no Jenner there. We breakfasted, we dined, we staid all night, and set out for Bath the next day. We would have come on to Berkeley, but we were afraid you might not be there. I am afraid it will not be in my power to come and see you, though I wish it much. I shall be obliged to take Southampton in my way home. Are the hedgehogs so saucy as to refuse coming without coming for them? See if you can coax them. We are alive here. The downs look like a beehive. Let me hear from you. Mrs. Hunter gives her compliments to you.

Yours,
J. Hunter.

Bath, 18th.

My letter was sent to your friend in Bristol by the coach, but perhaps the coachman forgot to deliver it.

When he came back from his enforced rest at Bath, Hunter again took up his experiments on vital heat.

XVI.

Dear Jenner,—I wrote to you twice from Bath since I saw you, and have had no answer to either; what the devil is become of you? I have got your candlesticks: to where shall I send them? Let me know by return of post; and all the news you can.

Yours,
John Hunter.

Nov. 6, 1777.

XVII.

Dear Jenner,—I have sent you the candlesticks as you desired. I hope you will like them. They cost five pounds and a shilling; so I owe you four shillings. I have received the hedgehogs. If you have time, see their natural winter haunts. . . . Observe their heat; you may do all this in a very few minutes. Observe the fluidity of the blood, by comparing it with another that has been kept warm for a few days. I have heard of Mr. Cattgal's collection of fossils, and not till I came to London; I suppose he will not sell any. I shall think of your lymphatics; and if I can pick up a preparation or two, I will. I am sorry you did not get my first letter, as we intended to go to Berkeley with you, but did not choose to come without an answer, as it was possible you might not be at home. I have seen your old master, who has given me the use of a very curious bone: I hope he will give it me altogether.

Dear Jenner, yours,
JOHN HUNTER.

Nov. 23rd.

XVIII.

DEAR JENNER,—I am always plaguing you with letters, but you are the only man I can apply to. I put three hedgehogs in the garden, and put meat in different places for them to eat as they went along; but they all died. Now I want to know what this is owing to: therefore I want you to find out their haunts, and observe, if you can, what they do: if they make a warm place for themselves; if they have any food by them, &c. I would have you kill one, and see its heat. . . . In short, make what observations you can. Let me hear from you when you have nothing else to do.

Yours,

J. HUNTER.

XIX.

DEAR JENNER,—Your letter of December has lain before me ever since I received it, to put me in mind that it was not answered. I am glad you liked the candlesticks: I thought them pretty. The fossils were none of the best; but I know you did not make them, therefore it is not your fault. The particular one you put the ♀? on is only the cast of a bivalve. I wish I had seen E.'s collection. I am matching my fossils, as far as I can, with the recent. Have you made any experiments with the hedgehogs, and can you send me some this spring? for all those you sent me died, so that I am hedgehogless.

Mr. Luders sent me the bone; it is a very curious one; whether he will let me keep it or no I do not know. I received yours by Mr. Jones, with the bird. I thank you for thinking of me. Frogs live an amazing while after they are dead; as also all animals of that tribe. The directions I gave you about the blackbirds were, when you have a blackbird's nest, viz., with four young ones, take one and put it bodily into spirit by the head, extending the wings and legs. Observe when the feathers begin to sprout; then take another, and serve it in the same way ; then a third, and a fourth, so as to get a series of the growth of the feather ; but the last, or fourth, must not be so old as the feathers to cover other parts where feathers do not grow. This you will better understand when you come to make the trial. I have a picture of Bassan's that I lent a poor devil three guineas upon : he died and never redeemed the picture. I intend sending it to you : it is a good deal damaged, but some of the figures are very good. Get a frame for it, and hang it in a strong light. There are some experiments of mine publishing in the Philosophical Transactions, which I will send you with the picture ; accept them as a remembrance of the trouble I put you to. Let me hear from you when convenient. Mrs. Hunter desires her compliments to you.

I am, dear Jenner,
Your most obedient and most humble servant,
JOHN HUNTER.

LONDON, *March* 29, 1778.

XX.

DEAR JENNER,—I received yours by Dr. Hicks, with the hedgehog alive. I put it into my garden : but I want more. I will send you the picture, but by what conveyance ? or to what place ? I have a picture by Barrett and Stubbs. The landscape, by Barrett ; a horse frightened at the first seeing of a lion, by Stubbs. I got it for five guineas. Will you have it? I have a dearer one, and no use for two of the same masters: but do not have it excepting you would like it, for I can get my money for it.

I am glad you have got blackbirds' nests. Let me know the expense you are at, for I do not mean the picture to go for anything, only for your trouble.

Ever yours,
J. H.

N.B.—I should suppose the hedgehogs would come in a box full of holes all round, filled with hay, and some fresh meat put into it.

The next three letters, of the summer of 1778, were written when Jenner was crossed in love.

XXI.

Dear Jenner,—I don't know when I wrote to you last. I do not know if I thanked you for the cider. The hedgehogs came, with one dead, which was a female, which I made a preparation of. I have since got the blackbirds, which I think will do vastly well. I have not yet sent the picture; it is packed up ready to go, and shall be sent immediately.

I was told the other day that you was married, and to a young lady with considerable fortune. I hope it is true, for I do not know anybody more deserving of one. Let me know whether it is so or not. I hope you keep an account of all expenses. What is become of your paper on lead in cider? Let me have it, and

I will send it to the Medical Society. How do the fossils go on?

XXII.

August 30th.

Dear Jenner,—I hope this winter to be able to get you some preparations of the eye and lymphatics; but Hewson's preparations are to be sold this month; now perhaps for four or five pounds some preparations may be picked up. If you have no objection to throw away so much money, let me know, and what subjects you would like best. I shall give you some commissions about heat, cold, &c.

Yours,
John Hunter.

XXIII.

Dear Jenner,—I own I was at a loss to account for your silence, and I was sorry for the cause. I can easily conceive how you must feel, for you have two passions to cope with, viz., that of being disappointed in love, and that of being defeated; but both will wear out, perhaps the first soonest. I own I was glad when I heard you was married to a woman of fortune; but "let her go, never mind her." I shall employ you with hedgehogs, for I do not know how far I may trust mine. I want you to get a hedgehog in the beginning of winter, and weigh him; put him in your garden, and let him have some leaves, hay, or straw to cover himself with, which he will do ; then weigh him in the spring and see what he has lost. Secondly, I want you to kill one in the beginning of winter, to see how fat he is, and another in spring, to see what he has lost of his fat. Thirdly, when the weather is very cold, and about the month of January, I could wish you would observe their heat. . . . So much at present for hedgehogs. I beg pardon,—examine the stomach and intestines. If Hewson's things go cheap, I will purchase some that I think proper for you; those you mention will, I am afraid, be everybody's money and go dear.

Ever yours,
J. HUNTER.

LONDON, *September* 25, 1778.

There are yet six more letters that were written before 1783; I put them here. A few letters, written in or after 1783, had best be put in the next chapter, with the events of 1783–1793.

XXIV.

LONDON, *November* 9, 1778.

DEAR JENNER,—I received yours, with the eel. The spawn of the salmon was lost. I shall send you back the eel again, with the liver, stomach, and gut removed, and nothing left but a fringe which passes down the sides of the backbone, which I took, and still take to be the spawn ; but I never saw any difference in it at any time of the year ; and this one you have sent is similar to all I have yet seen. I think your stopping the eels a good plan, if you can ; but I should suspect they would be more slippery than hedgehogs. I do not know if hedgehogs burrow. About a month hence examine another, and compare him with your notes and memory also. Examine his heat, &c. ; a month after that, another, &c. I like your experiment with the toad and snake ; but bury them rather deeper, and let the ground be kept moist about them, especially in summer. I shall keep all your letters, but I expect in the end all your notes. I like your friend Ludlow much ; he is a lively sensible fellow. I have got a few preparations for you ; I am getting them put into a little order for you before I send them. Are there no bats in the old castle of Berkeley? I should like similar experiments to be made upon them to those of the hedgehog. Mrs. H. desires her compliments to you.

Believe me to be, most sincerely yours,

J. HUNTER.

XXV.

DEAR JENNER,—What are you doing? How do the hedgehogs get on? How cold are they in the winter? &c., &c. Let me hear from you. I have not yet sent the preparations for you. I have added an eye to one of them of my own making.

Yours,

J. HUNTER.

LONDON, *January* 16, 1779.

JOHN HUNTER

XXVI.

Dear Jenner,—I thank you for the trouble you have taken. I do not see another experiment to be made with the hedgehogs, but one: get a piece of meat into the stomach of one during the very cold weather, and kill him twenty-four hours after, to see if it is digested, which I have done with lizards. This may be difficult, but suppose he was made lively in a warm room, and then fed, and put out into the cold immediately, with a little hay over him. If this does, two or three may be served in the same way, and kill them at different distances respecting time. Observe their breathing when in the cold; if possible, the quickness of the pulse and fluidity of the blood. If you chance to get more than you use, I would take a few to put into my garden, to walk about in the evenings.

Is there no chance to see you in London this winter? Do come and see us. I shall send you a paper of mine on the free martin, also one to Ludlow. If a good deal of that air in the hog's guts could be collected, see if a candle would burn as large in it as in common air. I had a letter from Mr. Cheston, of an ossified thoracic duct; I wish he would let me have it. You see how greedy I am. You will hear from me soon.

Ever yours,
John Hunter.

HUNTER AND JENNER

XXVII.

Dear Jenner,—I have not troubled you with any letter this long time, nor have I heard from you. This moment, I do not know if I sent you the butterflies; if they are not sent, they shall this week. I want you to pursue the experiments on the heat of the hedgehog this winter; and if you could send me a colony of them, I should be glad, as I have expended all I had, except two: one an eagle ate, and a ferret caught the other. Mrs. Hunter and I were at Bath the other day, and came home by way of Gloucester; we wished much we could have staid a day, to have waited on you. Let me hear from you soon.

I am, dear Jenner,
Yours,
John Hunter.

London, *Nov.* 8, 1779.

XXVIII.

Dear Jenner,—This very evening I was going to write to you, when behold a basket came with peafowls, lizards, and birds' legs. I know nothing of the natural history of the viviparous lizard, but shall ask Sir Joseph Banks, who, I dare say, knows; but I should like to have them when with young, therefore beg you will give a genteel reward to those who will bring you several; and let me know in what situations they are commonly found, that I may employ others to hunt for me. How did the puppy and you agree?

JOHN HUNTER

Last night I looked over all your letters, to see the one giving me the account of the porpoise, but I could not find it; therefore I must beg your account of them, and the milk, &c., which I hope you will send soon. Lord Berkeley has not sent for his dog. Have you had any account of the bustard?

Monday morning has produced nothing new, so good-day to you.

J. Hunter.

March 4th.

XXIX.

Dear Jenner,—I could not buy a single preparation for you, they all went so dear. Injections of the lymphatics of a turtle sold for guineas, an eye not injected for 15 shillings, and so of all the rest. I know of a young man who wants to sell some of his preparations; if they are good and cheap I mean to purchase them for you, but not if they are not a good bargain. I want two or three hedgehogs to complete my expt. upon living sleeping animals. Let me know how the world goes with you.

I am, dear Jenner,
Yours,
John Hunter.

London, October 30th.

HUNTER AND JENNER

These wonderful letters are above the level of commonplace praise, with its italics and notes of admiration. We seem to read them over Jenner's shoulder. There is another letter, not to Jenner, more notable than any of them; for it was written only a few months before Hunter died, to a friend in Africa. The spelling of it has been left unchanged :—

DEAR SIR,—I was favoured with your letter of September 31, informing me of 2 birds called the Habanah being shipped on board the Bull Dog, but unluckly the birds died on the passage home. I consider myself as equally obliged to you for thinking of me and taking so much trouble. I was sorry at the loss of your insects, after all the trouble of collecting them, but I hope you will be more succesfull in future. I mentioned your proposal to Sir Joseph Banks of having a gardiner sent out, he told me he had had a letter or letters to that same purpose from you, therefore I suggested, if it was a scheme he approved of, he could settle that with you, therefore I dropd it. There is one thing I wish very much to have settled in Natural History, which is the Natural History of Swallows; they breed with us in the summer, and leave us in the winter, and it is what becomes of them in our winter; now if they are with you in the winter, and if they should breed with you in that season, it would be a proof that they are birds of passage, and upon the same principle you should have many more in the winter than in the summer, as there are four or five different species in this country in the summer. I should like to have specimens of those that are with you in the winter. I remember seeing swallows in Portugal in the winter, but I cannot say what species they were. It would hardly be possible to get ostrach eggs just going to hatch, and to crush the shell and put them into proof spirits to preserve them till they came to England. If a Foal camell was put into a tub of spirits and sent, I should be glad. Is it possible to get a young tame lion, or indeed any other beast or Bird? If camelions were sent it should be in the spring, as then one could feed them with Flys through the summer. Are there any cuckews with you? We have none in the winter. I want everything respecting the Bee tribe, such as wasps with their nests, also hornets with theirs. They are a very large tribe. I would have sent you a paper I wrote on the anatomy of the Bees which was published in the Philosophical Transactions, but upon enquiry I found that it would cost you more than it is worth. I am a subscriber to the African Society, but I have not heard of the cachuna things &c., but as I cannot always attend, they may have come without my knowing it. I consider myself very much obliged to you for your attention to me, and I wish I knew how I could return it, which would give me pleasure. I hope you keep your health well.

I am, dear Sir,
Your much obliged and humble servant,
JOHN HUNTER.

January 15, 1793.

There could be no better example than this letter of the vehement energy of Hunter's life. In his old age, full of suffering, over-worked, and close to death, he was yet writing to Africa for swallows, ostrich-eggs, a camel, cuckoos, a young lion, everything respecting the bee tribe, chameleons, and any other beast or bird.

VI

London, 1783–1793.—Leicester Square

" My life is in the hands of any rascal who chooses to annoy and tease me."

TOWARD the end of Hunter's life, his attacks of angina occurred so often and came from such slight provocation, that he was not for one day free from pain. Of one such attack (April, 1785) Home writes :—

" I was with him during the whole of this attack, and never saw anything equal to the agonies he suffered ; and when he fainted away, I thought him dead. These affections at last seized him when lying in bed, and in his sleep, so as to awaken him. . . . The exercise that generally brought on the spasms was walking, especially on an ascent, either of stairs or rising ground ; the affections of the mind, that brought them on, were principally anxiety or anger ; the anxiety about the swarming of a hive of bees brought it on ; the anxiety lest an animal should make its escape before he could get a gun to shoot it, brought it on; even the hearing of a story would bring it on; anger brought on the same complaint, and he could conceive it possible for that passion to be carried so far as totally to deprive him of life. But what was very extraordinary, the more tender passions of the mind did not produce it; he could relate a story which called up the finer feelings, as compassion, admiration for the action of gratitude in others, so as to make him shed tears; yet the spasm was not excited."

The winter of 1789-90 left its mark on him for the rest of his life, after a severe attack of giddiness with loss of memory and derangement of vision :—

"His recovery from this indisposition was less perfect than from any of the others; he never lost entirely the oblique vision; his memory was in some respects evidently impaired; and the spasms became more constant. He never went to bed without their being brought on by the act of undressing himself; they came on in the middle of the night; the least exertion in conversation after dinner was attended by them; he felt therefore obliged to confine himself within a certain sphere of action, and to avoid dining in large companies. Even operations in surgery, if attended with any nicety, now produced the same effects. . . . His coachman being beyond his time, or a servant not attending to his directions, brought on the spasms. . . . In the beginning of October, 1792,

JOHN HUNTER

one at which I was present was so violent that I thought he would have died."

Each attack might be the last; and he had no desire, natural or philosophical, of death. Once, when he spoke his thoughts concerning it, somebody asked him if it were true that his own brother, when he came to die, praised its ease and pleasantness; and he answered, "Aye, 'tis poor work when it comes to that." He had saved no income for his wife and children, and he could not insure his life; his museum must be sold to keep them after he was dead, or, if not sold to Government, then bought under the hammer; and the greater part of his writings was still in manuscript. To add to his distress, the pathology of angina pectoris was not understood, and the disease itself was scarce recognised. He never solved the problem of his own case. They treated him with a host of remedies, many unpleasant, all inefficient. And he was by occupation and by character exposed to the fullest penalties that angina can exact.

He watched and noted himself, talked over his symptoms, quoted them in his lectures:—

"Each symptom was described at the time it occurred, and either noted by himself, or dictated to me when Mr. Hunter was too ill to write; they will therefore be found more accurately described than in ordinary cases."

And Home, after this preface, gives twenty quarto pages to a minute account of the case. Light became painful to him, and everything looked yellow; upright objects appeared sloping, things near seemed far off; he felt only four feet high, and as if he had no head; dreams were as real as anything else, and he slept hardly two hours in the twenty-four; so the notes of his illness in 1789 run on, written or dictated by Hunter himself. To the very last, three days before he died, he was still watching himself:—

"I had a very long conversation with him, on the Sunday, in which we were insensibly led to his complaint; a subject of all others the most interesting to his friends, and on which he was never backward in conversing. He was willing to hear every argument against the probable existence of an organic infirmity; but it was easy to see that his own opinion remained the same. Nor did he fail, on this occasion, to revert to the effect it had on his temper." (Adams.)

In 1783, the year his brother died, John Hunter's lease of the house in Jermyn Street came to an end. He was now fifty-five, had been twenty years in practice, and fifteen years surgeon to St. George's Hospital; and his professional income, which up to 1774 never reached a thousand pounds, had risen to about five thousand. But he saved little of it, always investing his savings, a most unprofitable investment, in his collection: till it outgrew and over-ran the house in Jermyn Street, and he must move elsewhere. So he bought the twenty-four years' lease of a large house on the east side of Leicester Square, and, with the house, he bought the ground behind it, and a house in Castle Street, now part of Charing Cross Road. On the ground between the two houses, he built a suite of rooms and a great museum. It was a terribly bad bargain; he spent altogether nearly £6,000; he died in 1793, and to the end of the lease, in 1806, his collection was still where he had left it. But he must find room for the work of his hands, and a house worthy of the greatness of his practice, without waste of time and temper over house-hunting. He began to build at once, and had to wait till 1785 before all the building was finished.

We owe to Dr. James Finlayson our knowledge of the cost of the establishments in Leicester Square and at Earl's Court. Seven years ago,[1] he published portions of an account-book kept by William Clift, whose story is told in Chapter IX. So soon as Hunter died, Clift's first care was to keep things together, and to mount guard over the vast store of preparations and of manuscripts. He made the first entry in his accounts on the day of Hunter's death; and added to them an estimate of the almost ruinous expenditure of his later years. Behind the great house, with its four tall drawing-room windows opening on the Square, lay the lecturing-theatre, and the meeting-room or salon, the "Conversazione Room." Above the theatre and the salon was the Museum, a long galleried room, fifty-

[1] See *British Medical Journal*, 1890, i. pp. 738, 865.

LONDON, 1783-1793

two feet by twenty-eight, lighted from the top. The house beyond, in Castle Street, was used for dissections, preparation of specimens, printing, and all the general work of the Museum. In the Royal College of Surgeons, there is a sketch by Clift of the ground-floor of the Leicester Square buildings. He marked on it, in his love of Hunter, everything: where Mrs. Hunter's sedan-chair stood in the hall, where the clock, Hunter's sofa-bed in the back parlour, the Reynolds portrait and the big Zuccarelli cartoons in the salon, the drawbridge to admit carriages from the square into the stables, the yard where they kept the whale's skull, and the spot "where Mr. Huger met the Irishman," and every least detail of the arrangement of the furniture.

After Hunter's death, his great rambling mansion, three blocks thrown into one, passed through many hands. Till 1806 the Museum was still filled with his collection. Later, the premises were used as a gallery for the exhibition and sale of pictures, then as a Museum of the Mechanical Arts and National Manufactures, then (1874) as the Headquarters of the Middlesex Volunteer Artillery. And there is a tradition that Stevenson drew from them his picture of the house and museum of Dr. Jekyll.[1]

---

[1] The house is No. 28, on the east side of the Square, immediately next the south side of the Alhambra. At the present time (Sept., 1897) the premises are in course of demolition. The front of the house is hidden by a hoarding covered with advertisements, leaving visible only the fine mouldings on the top of the front. The central buildings are

JOHN HUNTER

It was a ruinous bargain, to spend £6,000, with a lease of only twenty-four years, on vast premises that would not sell for half that money. But he liked things done in the grand style, and kept a costly establishment. We have Clift's account of it all:—

"Notwithstanding the very large eating and drinking establishment on the preceding Pages; and the Host of Tradesmen employed, as the Bills hereafter will show, together with the large outstanding Debts, and money borrowed at Interest, of Gawler; old Mr. Clarke, Cuttler, of Exeter Change; of Hannah Appleby; of Mrs. Home, etc., and the great expense of increasing and supporting the Museum, and the large prices he gave for individual Preparations; and the large sum he expended in building the stabling, Conzersatione and lecture room, and Museum over them, with an immense Skylight over the yard to protect the Whale's Skull—of perhaps 500 superficial feet of Glass—with Entrance Galleries, &c., and the expensive but ineffectual *Empyreal* warm-Air Stoves by Jackson & Moser, with the Great Draw-bridge and slope made to let the Chariot down from the Street, and consequent necessary great alterations of the House, in Windows and Doorways for that purpose— at more than £6,000—on a lease of about twenty years. Notwithstanding the expence of keeping up

---

almost swept away. The Castle Street house (it was No. 13) is half pulled down, just an empty shell still left. The last occupants of the Leicester Square house were Messrs. Hawke, music publishers.

two establishments of Coaches and 6 Horses, Coachmen and Footmen, &c., &c.; Mr. Hunter was always on the look-out for bits of Land adjoining to his previous possessions at Earl's Court; and for bargains, many of them of *little* use, as an enormous Electrifying apparatus; a splendid but unfinished Air Pump invented by the Earl of Bute, together with a grand Chemical furnace and apparatus by ditto; a magnificent and highly finished Turning Lathe which was made for the great Duke of Cumberland; several beautiful and large pieces of Tapestry; Chinese Ivory puzzle-Balls; Armour of all sorts and kinds; an acre of Landscapes and figures painted by Zuccarelli as models for Tapestry, which covered the walls and doors of the Conversatione room; as well as a very fine collection of proof prints by Hogarth, Strange, Woollett, Sharp—of the latter artist several hundred pounds' worth; besides Chinese Josses and beautiful nodding mandarines; and several original pictures by Zoffany, Vandevelde, Xuys, Ostade, Teniers, Stubbs, &c., &c. The large number of animals, both tame and wild, that were kept both in London and at Earl's Court, which consisted not only of presents, but often considerably expensive purchases; serve only to make one Wonder that Mr. Hunter had not died more involved, or that he should have left anything for the support of his family after all his Debts had been liquidated."

Clift's list of Hunter's household is of amazing length :—

JOHN HUNTER

In the year 1792 Mr. Hunter's Family consisted of the following Number of Persons :—

In Leicester Square.

1. John Hunter, Esq., F.R.S.
2. Mrs. Anne Hunter, his Wife, elder Sister to Everard Home, Esq.
3. John Hunter, the Son; from St. John's College, Cambridge.
4. Agnes Hunter, the Daughter (now Lady Campbell).
5. Everard Home, Esq. (afterwards Sir Everard Home, Bt.).
6. Thomas Nicol, Esq., Son of the Rev. Dr. Nicol, Articled Studt.
7. Dr. Edward Bradley, of Alresford, Hants, House Pupil, 1 yr.
8. Mr. Francis Kinloch Huger, N. Carolina, House Pupil, 1 yr.
9. Mr. James Smith, of Ecclefechan, N. Brit[n], House Pupil, 1 yr.
10. Mr. Henry Jenner, nephew of Dr. Jenner, Berkeley, 1 year.

Servants.

11. Robert Adcock, Butler (after Mr. Dewell).
12. Ann Martin, from Southampton, House Keeper.
13. Elizabeth Roby, from Rochester, Lady's Maid.
14. Mr. Hunter's Coachman, Joe.

LONDON, 1783–1793

15. Mr. Hunter's Footman, John.
16. Mrs. Hunter's Coachman, James Goodall.
17. Mrs. Hunter's Footman, George Smith.
18. Mary Edwards, from Llanbeder, cook (Ann Denny, do.).
19. Martha Jones, House-Maid.
20. Little Peggy, do. (*a great laugher*).
21. Mrs. Long (Constant Needlewoman).

In Castle Street House.

22. Robert Haynes, Dissecting room and Lectures.
23. Elizabeth Adam, House and Door-Keeper.
24. William Clift, Museum and Amanuensis.

At Earl's Court, Kensington.

25. Peter Shields, Gardener.
26. Mrs. Shields, House-Keeper and Dairy Woman.
27. Betty, Laundry-maid. (*Butter would not melt in her mouth, but somehow she became enceinte by an equally bashful Kensington sweetheart.*)
28. Tom Barton, Carter.
29. Scotch Willie, Half-witted, employed in the fields.
30. Old David, Head Under Gardener, Hot-houses, &c.
31. Alexander, Out-door Gardener, and Spring-guns.
32. Woman to weed in Garden, and fetch the Cows.

33. Tom Barton's Wife, Assistant-Laundress.

---

34. Monsieur St. Aubin, Draughtsman, in House, 1 yr.

35. Mr. Dupré, Secretary for Surgeon and Inspector Genl.

36. Mr. Walker, Teacher of Elocution to John.

Outdoor Tradesmen, nearly constant employ.

37. Sawyer Carpenter in London.
38. ,, Carpenter at Earl's Court.
39. Piper, Bricklayer and Mason, Earl's Court.
40. Benjamin Harris, Blacksmith, Castle Street.
41. Jas. Weatherall, Cabinet Maker and Joiner, Upholsterer.
42. Painters and Glaziers, Hot and Green Houses.
43. ⎫ Printers, nearly constant in Castle Street.
44. ⎬ John Richardson, Compositor ; Long, Press-
45. ⎭ man.

— Mrs. Hunter's Livery Stable Keeper, Mr. Rand, Golden Sq.

— Cart, Harness, and Collar-maker, Earl's Court.

— Farrier, nearly Constant, from Under-ground Stables.

— Stewardson, *an old Butler, a constant Visitor.*

" From the above List, which is but Imperfect, and Several of the Master Tradesmen sending Two or more men, besides occasional helpers to the Coachmen, Gardeners, and in the Grounds, &c., *there were never fewer* than 50 Persons daily provided for at Mr. Hunter's expence, exclusive of the House-Pupils, who paid for their Board."

This list throws light on the fashionable side of John Hunter's life. So near his death as 1792, in spite of his enfeebled health, he would keep Clift writing while he dictated, from seven to eleven at night, "and sometimes an hour or two later;" and Sir Richard Owen, who married William Clift's daughter, has said, "My father in law has described to me the scene he often stayed to witness with sleep-laden eyes, when the master could no longer dictate, and issued from his study on the ground floor, to take his much-needed repose, on one of Mrs. Hunter's reception-nights, with difficulty stemming the social stream on the staircase."

In August, 1784, Everard Home came back from Jamaica, where he had been staff-surgeon.[1] He says that Hunter appeared to him much altered in his looks, and much older than his years:—

"I found Mr. Hunter now advanced to a very considerable share of private practice, and a still greater share of the public confidence. His collection had

[1] "I returned to England from Jamaica, where at the close of the war I had been appointed staff-surgeon. Sir Archibald Campbell, the governor, coming home, gave me leave of absence on account of my health, and allowed me to attend him. We arrived in August, 1784, and I was permitted to exchange upon half-pay." Sir Archibald Campbell was brother of Captain, afterward Sir James, Campbell, who married Hunter's daughter Agnes.

increased with his income. In this he was materially assisted by the friendship of Sir Joseph Banks, who not only allowed him to take any of his own specimens, but procured him every curious animal production in his power, and afterwards divided between him and the British Museum all the specimens of animals he had collected in his voyage round the world. To his friends the honourable Mr. Charles Greville and Mr. Walsh he was also under particular obligations.

"Drawing materials from such ample sources, standing alone in this branch of science, and high in the public estimation, he had so much attention paid to him that no new animal was brought to this country which was not shown to him; many were given to him; and of those that were for sale he commonly had the refusal. Under these circumstances his collection made a progress which would otherwise have been impossible."

By his brother's death in 1783, Hunter was left unrivalled in anatomy; and by the death of Percivall Pott in 1788 he became the first surgeon in London. For these last few years he bore a stupendous burden of work. As Thackeray says of Swift, he "tore through life": and the two men are not unlike in temperament and suffering. His letters to Jenner, about 1783–84, take up fresh subjects without dropping those of former years. Two of them are concerned with a case of colour-blindness: one giving minute directions how Jenner is to test his patient's judgment of colours and shades, the other worth quoting as an example of Hunter's strange affection for a sham sort of philosophy :—

DEAR JENNER,—I received your's, with the heron's legs. Could you get a live heron or bittern— or see how they make the noise—and send them to me ? I will pay expenses.

By the by, you were to have sent me some hedgehogs. I am putting my things into some order, and shall find some Don Saltero's for you.

My proof of the non-existence of matter is in colours, there being no such thing as a primary colour, every colour being a mixture of two, making a third. . . . All colours are compounds. But what are they compounds of ? Of nothing but themselves. And what are themselves ? Nothing. If there were three colours that were permanent (for with less than three we can hardly compound to any extent), which could not be produced from any compounding of colours, then I would say there is something immutable in matter, although metaphysicians might say this was only an immutable idea, or an idea of immutability ; but that is only applying abstract reasoning to matter, or what we call matter ; but when we see that there is no such thing as permanency in one species of matter, viz., light, and that it can be proved from the matter itself, it then comes more home to our understandings than all the reasoning in the world.—Yours always, J. H.

JOHN HUNTER

Other letters are about a discovery that Jenner made at this time—a new method of preparing tartar emetic [1]:—

I.

Nov., 1783.

DEAR JENNER,—I received yours, with the experiments on heat and colours, but have not had time to pay sufficient attention to the colours. I also received your little publication with the Tart. Emet. I have a great deal to say about it. First, do you mean to take out a patent? Do you mean to advertize it? or do you mean to let it take its chance? I approve of it much, and will do all in my power to promote the sale; but I would advise you to give it a new name, expressive either of the composition or of its virtues on the body, viz., sal antim., or sal sudorif., or sal antim. sudorif. I would also desire you to burn your book, for you will have all the world making it. Let me have your answer to all this.

Ever yours,
J. HUNTER.

II.

Dec., 1783.

DEAR JENNER,—I have delayed writing longer than

[1] "He had been often foiled and disappointed in practice by the uncertainty of the action of this very useful medicine, arising from the imperfection of its preparation. He therefore instituted some experiments for the purpose of obtaining one more regular in its strength, and consequently more uniform in its operation." (Baron's "Life of Jenner.")

LONDON, 1783-1793

I intended, and longer than what I should have done, and even now I do not know what well to write. I love a new name so well that I could have wished it had been christened. Mr. Jones informed me that there was a man of some fortune making experiments with the same view; he may hit on some method much better than the present, and which may or may not be as good as yours, or it may be thought to be as good. I asked Jones if he had any objection to have it advertised at his shop: he did not give me a direct answer, and he is now out of town. I should be glad to have a few of the printed accounts. I could send them to different people—to Black and Cullen, &c., among the rest. I like your experiment upon the dogs with it: if you make any more, let me have them. . . . Let me know what service I can be to you.

J. HUNTER.

III.

Jan., 1784.

DEAR JENNER,—I am puffing off your tartar as the tartar of all tartars, and have given it to several physicians to make trial, but have had no account yet of the success. Had you not better let a bookseller have it to sell, as Glass of Oxford did his magnesia? Let it be called Jenner's Tartar Emetic, or anybody's else that you please. If that mode will do, I will speak to some, viz., Newberry, &c.

JOHN HUNTER

You are very sly, although you think I cannot see it; you very modestly ask for a thermometer; I will send one, but take care those damned clumsy fingers do not break it also. I should be glad to have a particular account of the cuckoo, and, as far as possible, under your own eye. To put all matters out of dispute, if the cuckoo's eggs were taken out of the hedge-sparrow's nest in which they were laid, and put into another's, by human hands, there could be no supposition that the parent cuckoo would feed or take care of them. I also want some young ones. I had a series from you, but a moth got in among them, and plucked them. Let me hear from you when you can.

Yours,
J. Hunter.

IV.

Jan. 26, 1784.

Dear Jenner,—To show you how much I am pleased to hear from you, I sit down to acknowledge the receipt of yours this evening. Somebody before told me of your experiment on swallows; but you should not have made the same experiment on both the old and the young of the same nest, for you do not know whether it was the old or the young that returned. I have been for some time going to write to you, to inform you that there is a medical society set up here, who intend to give papers in medicine and surgery, and also to receive. I think your paper on the Tart. Emetic would make a good paper, and probably the one on the ophthalmia, which you may probably take a little more pains about. If you should like to have them published, I can communicate them. If your account of the cuckoo is not so full as you see it may be, keep it to another year, for I am in no hurry.

     I am, dear Jenner,
       Ever yours,·
        JOHN HUNTER.

v.

May 29, 1784.

DEAR JENNER,—You must excuse me if I am not very punctual in my answers; it is my loss, not yours. In my last but one you mention my having anything of the porpoise I wanted. . . I hope you have got the thermometer. I want the cuckoo cleared up: I am afraid it is now too late. I wish you would shoot an old one for me, and send its gizzard in spirits.

I wish you would draw out the process of making the tartar emetic. The physicians that I have given it to speak well of it as a more certain medicine than the other; however, I am afraid it will be too late for this year's publication; but put it to paper. Your paper must be published before you can think of being a member, and then we will stir for you.

       Ever yours,
        JOHN HUNTER.

JOHN HUNTER

In Hunter's time the possession of secret remedies (Letter I.) was not thought wholly disgraceful. Hunter would meet Plunkett, the cancer-curer, in consultation—"I have no objection to meet anybody"—and there is a good story of his meeting a famous quack, Taylor, of Whitworth, whom the Lord Chancellor Thurlow had got to see his brother, Thurlow, Bishop of Durham. Several members of the faculty, Hunter among them, met Taylor to consult over the Bishop's case. Hunter was late, and they asked Taylor to examine the case without delay; but he said he would do nothing till Jack Hunter came, for he had no opinion of anybody but him. When Hunter arrived, he took up a box of ointment that Taylor was using, and asked what the ointment was made of. Taylor turned to the Lord Chancellor, and said, "That's not a fair question; no, no, Jack, I'll send you as much as you please, but I won't tell you what it's made of." Jenner might have kept his method to himself; but he followed the advice of Hunter's second thoughts, and in June, 1784, his paper was read before the Society for the Promotion of Medical and Chirurgical Knowledge. It was in February of this year that the Society received Hunter's memorable paper on "Inflammation of the Veins."

The next year, 1785, was half wrecked by angina and gout together. He had his first severe attack in April; again, in May, he was taken ill, and on May 20 told Pitcairn that six weeks ago he had cut his hand examining the body of a patient who had died of hydrophobia, and that he had gone in fear of it for the last fortnight. In June he began to amend, but still had attacks of pain :—

"He continued very much in the same way till August, when he went to Tunbridge, and drank the waters for about a fortnight, without the least benefit, but rather conceived he was worse. From thence he hurried to Bath,[1] the first week in September, and drank the waters for four weeks, twice before breakfast and once at noon. Having drunk them for about a fortnight, he began to bathe every other night in the hot-bath, and on the intermediate nights put his feet into the hot-bath waters, and sometimes rode on horseback. After being there three weeks he did not find the least benefit ; but on Monday, the beginning of the fourth week, he found that his walking to the pump-room did not bring on the spasm as usual, and found also that he could extend his walk very

[1] *From Mrs. Hunter to Edward Jenner.*

BATH, *Sept.* 13, 1785.

DEAR SIR,—I take it for granted you will not be sorry to hear Mr. Hunter is so near you, though you will lament that want of health is the occasion. He has been tormented with a flying gout since last March, and we are come here in hope of some favourable crisis before the winter. He has been inquiring for the post to Berkeley, and I find within this hour that it goes off this evening ; as he is now asleep after dinner, I rather write myself than disturb his nap, to inform you of our being in your neighbourhood, and that Mr. Hunter will be glad to hear from you.

I am, dear Sir, your obedient Servant,

A. HUNTER.

considerably on that day; on Tuesday he was not quite so well, although when he compared that day with the preceding days, or rather months, he could say that he was better. This seemed to be a step gained. In this state he left Bath, and continued the same throughout the whole winter." (Home.)

Henceforth he must have some help in his practice and affairs: and from this time till 1792 Everard Home lived with him, helped him at operations, took any work that came at night, and attended to his general business; and in 1792 married, and took a house for himself only a few doors off.

The move into the new premises in Leicester Square was made in the summer of this same year 1785. Everard Home, William Bell, and a new assistant, Mr. André, all helped to move the preparations and store them in the new museum. There are two letters to Jenner, written a short time before Hunter moved house:—

I.

DEAR JENNER,—I am very much obliged to you for your attention to me. I will very readily give three guineas for the bustard, therefore give such orders as you think fit. I request the whole history of the cuckoos this summer from you. I have bought a house in Leicester-fields, and shall move this summer, when I shall be able to pick out some things for you. Give my compliments to Clench, and I hope to see him before he sets out for Newfoundland; if I do not, let him think of the white hares, to tame a buck and doe, and send them to me. Let me know in your next what you are doing. I hope to see you in London in about two years hence, when I shall be able to show you something.

I am, dear Jenner,
Ever yours,
JOHN HUNTER.

When the bustard arrives, I will write you.

II.
April 22 (1785).

DEAR JENNER,—I have received the bustard safe, as also the bones. Your friend Mr. Hazeland has been very kind, for which I wrote to him and thanked him; but when you see him or write to him, express the same, as an indirect thank is better than a thousand direct ones. Are hedgehogs in great plenty? I should like to have a few. You must pursue the cuckoo this summer. I am employed building, moving, &c. I wish this summer was well over. When I am fitted up, I hope you will come and see me.

Ever yours,
J. HUNTER.

The year thus interrupted by illness and by house-moving was yet the *annus mirabilis* of Hunter's life as a surgeon; in December he performed for the first time the operation for aneurysm which will always be associated with his name—tying the main artery high up above the disease, and leaving the collateral circulation to nourish the parts beyond the ligature. This operation, which has saved thousands of limbs and lives, was the result of work in many fields of thought; in it he united a whole multitude of facts from anatomy, physiology, clinical experience, *post mortem* examinations, and experiments on animals; it remains one of the best deductions ever made in surgical practice. And to show that he was not over-adventurous in thus altering the rules of his art, we have his own words concerning the operation :—

"In this account it may be supposed that I carry my notions too far; but it is to be understood that I only give my own feelings upon this subject, and I go no further in theory than I would perform in practice, if patients, being acquainted with the consequences of the disease, would submit to, or rather desire, the operation; nor do I go further than I now think I would have performed on myself were I in the same situation. Not that I would have it supposed that I would recommend this at large; I would have no one perform an operation that he is not clear about the propriety of himself. . . . Although I would perform the operation on all the arteries I have mentioned, and if I laboured under them myself would have them performed on me, yet I would wish every person to judge for himself, and not attempt an operation if he is fearful."

LONDON, 1783–1793

The next year, 1786, found and left Hunter less fit for work, yet ever engaged in it. From June to September, says Home, he was able to take a long walk slowly, but would have a slight attack of pain on the least exertion ; in October he was obliged always to use his carriage, because he could not walk fast enough to keep himself warm ; he had now given up wine, and was beginning to get fat from want of exercise. This was a year of much writing ; in the spring, he published his " Treatise on the Venereal Disease," and a few months later his " Observations on Certain Parts of the Animal Œconomy." Both these books were printed under his own supervision, at his own house, and thence published :—

" His reason for doing this was that before the Irish Union it was no infrequent proceeding with booksellers to send a copy of the manuscript, or else the proof sheets, of any valuable work to Dublin, where a cheap edition was hastily got up and imported to England so as to be ready for sale as soon as the original work ; by which means the author was deprived of the profits which would have accrued to him from a second edition being called for. This proceeding, however, gave great offence to the booksellers ; and as some of them were old friends, with whom he did not wish to quarrel, he gave the publication of the second edition of the 'Animal Œconomy' to Mr. Nicol, of Pall Mall, and Johnson of St. Paul's Churchyard." (Ottley.)

JOHN HUNTER

The Treatise, every page of it, was submitted to a committee of friends—Sir Gilbert Blane, Dr. Fordyce, Dr. David Pitcairn, and Dr. Marshall. It was a quarto volume of 398 pages, with plates, price a guinea. "The sale of it was rapid at first, from curiosity being artificially raised, as the papers of the day had announced that it was to throw all former productions at a humble distance"—(Jesse Foot)—and a second edition was published in 1788. He had spent an infinity of trouble over it, and had laid a heavy task on his four friends to give lucidity and style to what was laboured and obscure; unwilling, as he often said, that any future edition should make the first edition useless. A third edition was published, the year after Hunter's death, by Everard Home, with omissions and additions of his own invention.

The "Animal Œconomy," most characteristic of all Hunter's works, was a reprint of nine monographs already published in the Transactions of the Royal Society, with others added to them; a wonderful series of experiments and observations. A second edition was published in 1792, to which were added two more monographs and some more illustrations.

This same year, 1786, on the death of Mr. Middleton, Hunter was appointed Deputy-Surgeon-General of the Army. There are two letters about this time to Jenner:—

LONDON, 1783-1793

I.

Dear Jenner,—I have been long expecting a long letter from you, informing me of your method of curing ophthalmias, history of cuckoos, &c. I received your dog-fish; are you sure that the spawn or egg came from her? There were none in her; if it did, then there is a species of dog-fish oviparous. Let me hear from you soon.

Ever yours,
J. Hunter.

Sept. 7th.

II.

Dear Jenner,—I have all your letters before me, but whether I have answered any of them or not I cannot recollect. First, I thank you for your account of the cuckoo, and what further observations you can make I shall be glad to have them, or even a repetition of the former will be very acceptable. I received the bird: it is well known; but I look upon myself as equally obliged to you. I also received your cocks, which were very good. I have bought the print of Wright, viz., The Smiths, which is his best. There is one more I would have you have, I mean Sir Joshua Reynolds's print of Count Ugolino; it is most admirable, and fit only for a man of taste. We had a sale of bad pictures lately, but there were some good heads: I gave a commission for them for you, thinking they would come cheap, but unluckily there were some that saw their merit as well as I, and they sold above my commission. Pictures seem to be rising again. I will not send you yours till I hear from you.

I am told there is the skin of a toad in Berkeley Castle that is of prodigious size. Let me know the truth of it, its dimensions, what bones are still in it, and if it can be stolen by some invisible being. I buried two toads last August was a twelvemonth; I opened the grave last October, and they were well and lively.

Have you any queer fish? Write to me soon, and let me have all the news, &c., &c.

Anny sends, with little John, their compliments.

From yours, &c.,

JOHN HUNTER.

In 1787, Hunter communicated to the Royal Society three papers; one giving some experiments on the reproductive power of animals; another on the identity of species of the wolf, the jackal, and the dog; the third was his famous account of the structure and œconomy of whales. For the first of these papers, he had kept note for five years of the fertility of two similar animals under different conditions:—

"It may be thought by some that I should have repeated the experiment; but an annual expense of twenty pounds for ten years, and the necessary attention to make the experiment complete, will be a sufficient reason for my not having done it."

LONDON, 1783-1793

The second paper gives a glimpse of shops that have long vanished from the London streets—Mr. Brookes, who dealt in animals, and lived in the New Road; Mr. Gough, who sold birds and had a collection of animals on Holborn Hill; Mr. Bailey, bird merchant, in Piccadilly. And it shows how Hunter worked by correspondence, writing to any one who would answer a question or make an observation for him—Sir Joseph Banks, Lord Wilton, Captain Mears, Mr. Plaw of Tottenham Court Road, and Mr. Cameron of Titchfield Street, who had lived many years among the Cherokees.

The monograph on the "Structure and Œconomy of Whales" occupies more than sixty pages of Palmer's edition of Hunter's works. It begins with regret that his opportunities had been so few; yet he had examined or dissected several porpoises, two grampuses, two bottle-nosed whales, a rorqual, a narwhal, a spermaceti whale, and a large whalebone whale:—

"Such opportunities too seldom occur, because these animals are only to be found in distant seas, which no one explores in search of natural history; neither can they be brought to us alive from thence, which prevents our receiving their bodies in a state fit for dissection. Some of them are sought after as objects of profit; but gain being the primary view, the researches of the naturalist are only considered as secondary points, if considered at all. At the best, our opportunities of examining such animals do not often occur till the parts are in such a state as to defeat the purposes of accurate inquiry. The parts of such animals being formed on so large a scale is another cause which prevents any great degree of accuracy in their examination, more especially when it is considered how very inconvenient for accurate dissections are barges, open fields, and such places as are fit to receive animals or parts of such vast bulk.

"As the opportunities of ascertaining the anatomical structure of large marine animals are generally accidental, I have availed myself as much as possible of all that have occurred; and, anxious to get more extensive information, engaged a surgeon, at a considerable expense,[1] to make a voyage to Greenland in one of the ships employed in the whale fishery, and furnished him with such necessaries as I thought might be requisite for examining and preserving the more interesting parts, and with instructions for making general observations; but the only return I received for this expense was a piece of whale's skin, with some small animals sticking upon it."

In spite of the difficulties of his work, he found pleasure in dissecting such vast creatures :—

"In our examination of particular parts, we behold them with astonishment in animals so far exceeding the common bulk as the whale. Thus the heart and aorta of the spermaceti whale appeared prodigious, being too large to be contained in a wide tub, the

[1] It is said that Hunter paid £500.

aorta measuring a foot in diameter. When we consider these as applied to the circulation, and figure to ourselves that probably ten or fifteen gallons of blood are thrown out at one stroke, and moved with an immense velocity through a tube of a foot diameter, the whole idea fills the mind with wonder."

This year, 1787, he received the Copley medal of the Royal Society, and was elected a member of the American Philosophical Society. His immense collection was now at last arranged in perfect order in the new Museum, and he set aside two months in the year to show and explain it to visitors: October for the profession, May for the "noblemen and gentlemen who were only in town during the spring:" and this custom he observed for the rest of his life.

About this time, Sir Joshua Reynolds painted the portrait of him which is in the possession of the Royal College of Surgeons. Hunter had often been asked by his friends to sit for his portrait, but had refused: he did not wish that they should pay the hundred guineas for it, he could not well afford them himself, and he hated the business of sitting. But his friend William Sharp, the engraver, persuaded him; and Reynolds promised to paint a masterpiece. Hunter was a bad sitter, and the portrait came to be nearly finished without being successful; then one day Hunter, as he was sitting, fell into deep thought. Reynolds silently turned his canvas upside down, and sketched a new head between the legs of the figure he had already painted. Thus he obtained the fine contrast between Hunter and the things round him—the manuscripts, the jars containing preparations, and the dangling feet of the Irish giant's skeleton. On the occasion of each Hunterian Oration at the College, this picture is hung opposite the audience, and above the Orator. Then one sees it at its best, set for commemoration and oration : the image of Hunter, and the praise of him, are for the hour united to give one impression ; and that is the right way to see a portrait.

The friendship between Hunter and William Sharp is to be noted; for the two men were wholly unlike :—

" Poor Sharp, though a man of extraordinary talent in his art, was singularly devoid of common sense. He was a firm believer in the pretensions of the prophet Brothers, and in Joanna Southcote ; but at the same time a man of profligate habits. Hunter was a great admirer of his talents as an artist, and possessed a large portfolio of splendid engravings by Sharp and other eminent masters in the art. Sharp always considered his engraving of Hunter (the Reynolds portrait) as one of his happiest efforts, and was found poring over it with admiration forty years after he had executed it. Hunter took fifty copies of the engraving at two guineas each." (Ottley.)

The next year, 1788, Hunter had the pleasure of seeing through his own press, and publishing from his own office, a second edition of his two-year-old book, the first thousand copies having all been sold within twelve months. He published no other work this year; and suffered innumerable attacks of angina. He was still compelled, since he could not save money, to work for it :—

May, 1788.

"DEAR JENNER,—I have been going to write to you some time past, but business and a very severe indisposition for three weeks past has prevented me; but when two guineas rouse me, I cannot resist. He should be very temperate in eating, drinking, and exercise; eat no salt nor made dishes; drink no fermented liquors. . . . Your paper has been read, passed the Council, and is in print, for I had a proof sheet this day, and I have ordered fifty copies, twenty-five for you, and twenty-five for myself, to give to friends. . . . Mrs. Hunter's and my compliments to Mrs. Jenner.

I am, dear Sir,
Your most obedient Servant,
JOHN HUNTER.

At the end of the year, on the 22nd of December, Percivall Pott died, midway between the threescore years and ten and the fourscore years; and Hunter was now the head of his profession. Even Jesse Foot admits this: "I think I may affirm that his consultations were more in fashion than any other surgeon's, and that his range of practice was more extensive; that we heard more of the name of John

JOHN HUNTER

Hunter than of any other surgeon." And Adams gives a pleasant picture of the rush of practice that came to the big house in Leicester Square :—

"He had now arrived at the highest rank in his profession ; was consulted by all those surgeons who were attached to Mr. Pott during that gentleman's lifetime ; he was almost adored by the rising generation of medical men, who seemed to quote him as the schools at one time did Aristotle. . . . His town house was beginning to return all the sums it had cost him ; it was spacious, and exactly suited for his residence. The ground floor was occupied for professional purposes ; and such was the afflux of morning patients, that to find room for them the drawing-room sometimes was so suddenly deserted that the French grammar and other implements of instruction were left behind."

The premises in Leicester Square were used for many purposes. In the great house in front he saw his patients ; and Foot says he often came to them with signs of the dissecting room about him. There was a sofa-bed in his study, for his use when he was exhausted or in pain. The house at the back, facing into Castle Street, was used for dissections and museum work, and probably received, through a back-way, bodies brought for dissection ; and the place was duly marked on Clift's pen-and-ink sketch, "Where Mr. Huger (one of the house-pupils) met the Irishman," as if the Irish giant's skeleton had been brought back from Earl's Court to Leicester Square. The Castle Street house also contained a printing-room, and an office where Hunter's books were sold; Jesse Foot went to the warehouse in 1786, to buy the new book, and found his friend André folding up the sheets, and women stitching them. "Such are the ludicrous sports of Fortune. It is with infinite pleasure I am able to tell that he has found a retreat, secure from the perilous peltings of adversity, as domestic librarian to a nobleman." The central suite of rooms, below the Museum, was used for a sort of medical conversazione every Sunday evening during the winter; "they were regaled with tea and coffee," says Foot, "and treated with medical occurrences." It was also the meeting-place of the Lyceum Medicum Londinense, a medical society founded by Hunter and Fordyce in 1785; "a society for disputation," says Foot again, "where all were of the same opinion, and which consisted of the same members who visited his levée. The room was called Lyceum Medicum; galleries were erected round it, the president wore his hat on, and John Hunter was the patron." Dr. Newton Pitt's account of the two medical societies especially associated with Hunter is put at the end of this chapter.

In 1789, after fourteen years, Mr. Bell left Hunter's service, and went to Sumatra as an assistant-surgeon in the employ of the East India Company, "to improve his fortune, and to collect specimens in natural

JOHN HUNTER

history." Three years later he died of fever there.

This same year, 1789, Mr. Adair died; who thirty years ago had given Hunter his first appointment in the service. Hunter now succeeded him both as Surgeon-General and as Inspector-General. The salary of these two appointments was in time of war £1,200; he might seem to be at last free from all want of money; but if 1789 lightened one load, it made another more heavy:—

"About the beginning of December, in the evening, when at the house of a friend on a visit, he was attacked with a total loss of memory; he did not know in what part of the town he was, not even the name of the street when told it, nor where his own house was; he had not a conception of any place existing beyond the room he was in, and yet was perfectly conscious of the loss of memory." (Home.)

He regained his memory in half an hour; but a fortnight later he was attacked with giddiness, derangement of vision, and loss of sleep; and was ill for some weeks. His health was impaired from this time onward; "in the autumn 1790, and in the spring and autumn 1791, he had more severe attacks than during the other periods of the year, but of not more than a few hours' duration; in the beginning of October, 1792, one at which I was present was so violent that I thought he would have died."

Of three letters to Jenner in 1789, two are but a

LONDON, 1783-1793

few lines long, on Jenner's election to the Royal Society; the third speaks for itself:—

Jan., 1789.

DEAR JENNER,—I wish you joy; it never rains but it pours. Sooner than the brat should not be a Christian I will stand godfather, for I should be unhappy if the poor little thing should go to the devil because I would not stand godfather. I hope Mrs. Jenner is well, and that you begin to look grave now you are a father.

Yours sincerely,
J. HUNTER.

This year he gave to the Society for the Improvement of Medical and Chirurgical Knowledge his paper on Intro-susception;[1] and next year, 1790, that on Paralysis of the Muscles of Deglutition, with the method of feeding the patient through a tube. On Dec. 8, 1790, he writes to Jenner on some surgical questions, and adds, " I should be glad to employ you if I knew in what, but if anything comes across my imagination I will think of you. How does Mrs. Jenner do? Do you bring her to London? What family have you got? My compliments to Mrs. Jenner." Later, he writes, " What are you about? I have not heard of you or from you this long time. You must certainly be about some mischief that keeps

[1] For an account of this paper, see *British Medical Journal,* 1897, ii. p. 300, "An Interesting Document."

you so quiet. Let me know what you are doing, or else I will blow you, and have you brought to town as a criminal." And on Dec. 10, 1791, he writes again, asking for more hedgehogs, and urging Jenner and Mrs. Jenner to come to town.

In 1792, he was made a member of the Royal College of Surgeons in Ireland, and of the Chirurgico-Physical Society of Edinburgh, and a Vice-President of the new Veterinary College of London. This year he published in the Transactions of the Royal Society his observations on Bees—twenty years' work, which alone would have made his name memorable; and he was busy finishing his Treatise on the Blood, Inflammation, and Gunshot Wounds. But he was now growing old, more from illness than from age; and angina had got the upper hand of him. In 1787 he had obtained the help of an Assistant-Surgeon for his hospital work; in 1790, after nearly twenty years, he gave up lecturing. Everard Home became his Assistant-Surgeon; he took the lectures;[1] he even

---

[1] The advertisement of them, in the *World*, Sept. 4, 1790, says:

SURGERY AND ANATOMY.
On Monday, October the 4th,
At Seven o'Clock in the Evening,
Mr. Hunter's Course of Lectures on the Theory and Principles
of Surgery, will be begun and continued as usual.
The Lectures will be read this Winter by his Brother-in-Law,
Mr. Home.
At the same time will be opened the Rooms for
Practical Anatomy.
For particulars of the Lectures and Dissections, inquire at No. 13, Castle Street, Leicester Square.

began to write the monographs, "from materials furnished by Mr. Hunter."

I.

Dr. Newton Pitt, in his Hunterian Oration, Feb. 13, 1896, gave a most valuable account of the Medical Societies of Hunter's time. Unhappily there is only room here to reprint a small part of it; but the whole Oration should be studied for the light it throws on medical affairs in those days. It was published in the *Lancet*, May 9, 1896. He says of the Society for the Improvement of Medical and Chirurgical Knowledge:—

"This Society issued three volumes of Transactions between 1793 and 1812. The Society was founded by John Hunter and George Fordyce, senior physician to St. Thomas's Hospital, in 1783, which is the date of delivery of the first paper, but none were published till ten years after. The society originally consisted of nine members, with power to increase up to twelve, but not beyond; and only eighteen, whose names are given in the minute book, joined during the thirty years of its existence. They met once a month at Slaughter's Coffee-house, and after dinner read and discussed the papers. Members to be eligible were required to be living in the neighbourhood so as to attend regularly, and they were required to be physicians or surgeons of five years' standing, or to be on the staff of St. Bartholomew's, St. George's, Guy's, or St. Thomas's Hospital. The first volume of Transactions was published in 1793, the year of Hunter's death; and after 1812, when the last volume was issued, the society continued merely as a club of ten, who dined together once a month. They had been, according to their last secretary (Mr. Benjamin Brodie), a very exclusive society; and finally dissolved in 1818."

The Lyceum Medicum Londinense was very different, having a very large membership, mostly of men not yet qualified :—

"The society was established under the patronage of John Hunter and Dr. George Fordyce in January, 1785. The meetings were held every Friday evening from 8.30 p.m. to 11 p.m. between October and May, in Hunter's lecture-room. . . . The Royal College of Surgeons of England possess a copy of the rules of the society, and a list of members from the foundation to the date of publication, 1792, from which we learn the following particulars. The society consisted of honorary, corresponding, and ordinary members; the latter being divided up into three classes. The six honorary members were the following teachers: John Hunter, lecturer on Surgery in the Haymarket; George Fordyce, lecturer on Physic at Essex Street; William Saunders, lecturer on Physic at Guy's Hospital; William Osborn and Thomas Denman, lecturers on Midwifery at Leicester Square; and William Cruikshank, lecturer on Anatomy at the Hunterian Museum, Great Windmill Street (William Hunter's school). The corresponding members, 21, were teachers or members of hospital staffs in the country. The ordinary members were (1) those who had taken a qualification or were in practice, 78, including Baillie, Home, Babington, Adair, Abernethy, and Astley Cooper; (2) those, 314, who had attended a hospital, and one course of lectures on Anatomy and the practice of Physic; (3) those, only 7, who were commencing their studies. Those belonging to (1) and (2) were required in turn to read a dissertation which, on the following Friday, was read out by the President and discussed. The first hour of each meeting was devoted to the narration of medical cases. The society possessed a library, and presented a gold medal annually for the best dissertation on a set subject. Fines were inflicted on a member who left a meeting without publicly standing up and asking permission, and for each time he failed to attend the meetings until he had read a dissertation, after which he attended at his convenience. There was an entrance fee of a guinea."

The whole of Dr. Newton Pitt's Oration should be read. At the end of it, he quotes from a pamphlet, " Reflexions on a Letter addressed to the Governors of St. George's Hospital by John Hunter in 1792."

JOHN HUNTER

The writer, after abusing Hunter for his want of education, says—

"Your disputing societies, several varieties of lectures in a day, and a squint at an operation, are the fashionable attendances of the modern student. Since the Medical Tea-sipping Society was commenced, mankind has been classed to view the wonders of your museum, and the world indulged with a volume of your notions at the common price. It is ridiculous to observe how this tea-kettle invitation has spread. An apothecary may now take his tea gratis and have a game of whist for only the price of the cards every evening in the week, if he keeps a regular list of the bread-and-butter manufactories."

II.

Miss Baillie has kindly allowed me to print the following account of Mrs. Hunter, written by Mrs. Milligan, daughter of Matthew Baillie.

"I will begin my reminiscences with the account of Mrs. John Hunter, who, except my grandfather (Thomas Denman), is the earliest living link to remote times. She was born 1742, and remembered when a young child the panic at the rising of Charles Edward in 1745, and on hearing the people around her speak of where they should go for safety, she said that she had heard Heaven was a very good place to go to, and that she would like to go there. She married my Father's Uncle, the celebrated John

LONDON, 1783–1793

Hunter, and was very much distinguished in the Society of her day. She was very handsome, tall, and singularly dignified and ladylike in appearance, and she had a generally cultivated mind, with special gifts for poetry and music. . . . She had during the season a party on one regular day in the week, when in addition to her own, there were the attractions of her sister Miss Home, who had a beautiful voice, and sang charmingly. Her conversation was bright and sparkling, and her manners were gentle and unassuming. I have heard my Aunt Agnes speak of the celebrated people she met at Mrs. Hunter's, amongst whom she mentioned Lord Orford, Madame D'Arblay, Mrs. Elizabeth Carter (between whom and Mrs. Hunter was a personal regard) and also Mrs. Montague, whom my Aunt admired much. It may be supposed that many persons were desirous to join these assemblies, but Mrs. Hunter wished to keep them select, and knew well how to repress intruders. One lady was so anxious to obtain admission that she resorted to the expedient of sending to Mr. Hunter to bleed her, in the hope of thus producing an acquaintance, but I do not know whether the plan succeeded. Mrs. Hunter never entertained company after Mr. Hunter's death in 1793. His magnificent museum was bought by Government, and an annuity was purchased for Mrs. Hunter with the sum paid for it, so that tho' with limited means she had enough not only for comfort but for ladylike and suitable arrangements. Her beautiful daughter married

JOHN HUNTER

Captain, afterwards Sir James, Campbell; who tho' not rich promoted the purchase of the annuity, obviously to his own disadvantage.

"When I first remember Mrs. Hunter, which was in my earliest childhood, she was about 60, but there was still much to be admired in her appearance. She was delicately fair, and her features were delicate as well as her complexion. She was very tall and singularly dignified and ladylike in her appearance and manners, and her dress and everything about her had a stamp of refinement. When I first recollect her, her sister Miss Home lived with her, but tho' younger she died before Mrs. Hunter, who lived alone for many years before her death, which took place in 1821. She resided in a small house in Lower Grosvenor Street, in order to be near my father and mother, who showed her constant and affectionate attention. She was very kind to me.

"Lady Campbell afterwards married Colonel Charleywood, but had no children by either marriage. She was very beautiful, and was much admired for her charm of manner and sparkling conversation."

III.

From Mrs. Hunter to Mrs. Joanna Baillie.
LOWER GROSVENOR STREET,
Wednesday, Oct. 20th.

I have to thank you Dear Joanna for your kind note enclosing Miss Edgeworth's letter; which has been to me highly gratifying. I do not mean to answer it, because I have no wish to draw her into a correspondence, and which if she even were disposed to, I am unable to support; but I will thank you to say that her and her family's approbation gives me infinite pleasure, and that if I am alive when she next visits London, to see her and her sisters will be a real gratification to my feelings; her letter is better than complimentery, it is kind and Friendly. I had an opportunity yesterday to call on Lady C. She has been very unwell, and tho' now better looks thin and pull'd—poor soul! Your letter to Lady Byron went by 10 o'Clock, so I hope was in good time. I am afraid this rain will interfere with your Sister's labour of love, if her task be not finished with the Locksmiths. Give my love to her, I know no one I should prefer to her as an active agent in the service of Friendship.

I am but a shabby person; however, we scramble on thro' Weeks, and Months, somehow or other, as well as we can. . . . Adieu! Dear Joanna.

Ever yours very Affectionately,
ANNE HUNTER.

St. George's Hospital

"We are but beginning to learn our profession."

THE history of St. George's Hospital goes back to the year 1734, at which time John Hunter was six years old. The hospital arose out of a dispute among the supporters of the old Westminster Infirmary. This charity, founded in 1719 in Petty France, Westminster, and removed in 1724 to Chappell Street, was in 1733 compelled to move a second time; for the premises in Chappell Street were neither commodious nor wholesome. Two houses were offered to the subscribers; one was in Castle Lane, Pimlico, the other was Lord Lanesborough's house at Hyde Park Corner. There was vehement disputation over the two sites; finally, at a general meeting of the subscribers, it was resolved that the house in Castle Lane should be purchased for the infirmary. Hereupon the minority, having on their side all the physicians of the infirmary, and many of its most clearsighted friends, would have nothing to do with the scheme, and took a lease of Lanesborough House, "which on account of the strength of the building and the airiness of the situation is much more convenient to answer the ends of the charity." Having moved to Castle Lane, the infirmary grew and prospered; and in 1834 built for itself its present home in Broad Sanctuary, the Westminster Hospital. Thus, out of a most fortunate quarrel, one infirmary became two hospitals.

At a meeting of the supporters of the Lanesborough House scheme, held on October 19, 1733, committees were appointed to fit up Lanesborough House with all convenient speed for the reception of patients, and to draw up bye-laws for the management of it upon the model of St. Thomas's Hospital. Six physicians and three surgeons, all honorary, were elected; and a few days later, that the new venture might have the assurance of a great name, Cheselden was added to the list of surgeons. Henceforth many meetings were held—rules were framed, contracts made for stores, governors appointed, subscriptions received—from Dr. Mead and Sir Hans Sloane among others—and an attempt was made, but in vain, to obtain a part of the funds of the old infirmary.

On New Year's Day, 1734, Lanesborough House was opened for the admission of patients, with thirty beds. The board met every week at the hospital; the various committee meetings were held at the coffee-houses, to save the trouble of going out to Hyde Park

JOHN HUNTER

Corner, which was then almost country. Within two years, they had sixty beds instead of thirty, and the money was coming in fast. In 1735 came the chance of buying the freehold of Lanesborough House, with two houses near it belonging to the Dean and Chapter of Westminster, and two acres of the field adjoining the hospital to the south. The three houses they bought for £500; the land, after long delay, they bought in 1767 from Lord Grosvenor, on a lease of ninety-eight years at a peppercorn rent, so long as the premises should be occupied as a public hospital. Then they enlarged the building, and started afresh with two hundred beds. This was Hunter's hospital. In the years 1824—1834, the whole hospital was rebuilt from the designs of Mr. Wilkins, architect of the National Gallery and of University College. At the present time, it has three hundred and fifty-six beds, and serves a whole city that has grown round it. In the days of Hunter, Hyde Park Corner was on the horizon of London, Kensington was almost country, Earl's Court was "a hamlet two miles from London." There is in the Foundling Hospital a picture of St. George's Hospital, as it was in 1746. Hyde Park, in the foreground, is a stretch of fields or of common land; then comes a country road, and then the hospital, blank and isolated; there is but one other house visible, about a hundred yards away.

The outward form of the hospital is not more changed than its inner life; and if Hunter could see

ST. GEORGE'S HOSPITAL

it again now, he would wonder less at its material advancement than at the school that it has created. In his lifetime, there was no medical school, in our sense of the words. The physicians and surgeons had each of them their own pupils, who followed them, and saw what they could of the work of the other men ; the pupils were present at operations, consultations, and *post mortem* examinations; and here their privileges came to an end. For everything else they must go outside the hospital : "they have to go for their Anatomy to Windmill Street; for their Midwifery to Queen Street, Golden Square ; for their Chemistry, Materia Medica, and Practice of Physick to Leicester Fields." (1793.) There were no lectures given in the hospital ; no notes kept by the pupils, no special departments, no museum, no classes, no hospital examinations. When Hunter came on the staff in 1768, St. George's was but thirty-two years old, a new venture, having neither charter nor endowment nor tradition ; governed by borrowed rules. It had grown rapidly, and such quick growth endangers the stability of hospital life. His disputes with his colleagues were a phase of the development of the hospital, not a violation of any fixed and traditional order of administration. He found a young and hardly settled institution, six years younger than himself; he saw it slowly lose its first enthusiasm ; and then quarrelled with his colleagues for this very reason, that they would not do enough for the pupils of the hospital. There came a final stage of the quarrelling, wherein he appears in a less favourable light; but it remains true that he was fighting for things essential to the success of a great hospital; and he fought, literally, at the risk of his life. We are free to believe that for fifteen years, up to 1783, he worked fairly well with his colleagues; nor was his quarrel with the physicians, but only with the surgeons. To some of the staff, his passionate love of science was wholly unintelligible; to him, for example, who said that Hunter's museum was no more use than so many pigs' pettitoes. Yet they could bear with his superiority here; what galled them was the crowd of pupils that entered under him, not under them; the rush to go round the wards with him, and his name in everybody's mouth, his rough jokes at their expense, his outspoken contempt of their pathological doctrines. Neither Gunning nor Walker nor Keate was either a fossil or a failure; and Hunter's pre-eminence over them was won in fields outside surgery, and he wore his laurels with an aggressive air.

For a quarter of a century, he was surgeon to the hospital. When he came on the staff in 1768, the other surgeons were Cæsar Hawkins, William Bromfield, and John Gunning. Cæsar Hawkins retired in 1774, Bromfield in 1780. Later, Bromfield was opposed to Hunter's operation for aneurysm; and in his opposition was neither wise nor straightforward: unwise because he advised that no operation of any kind should be done for aneurysm, and backed this

ST. GEORGE'S HOSPITAL

advice by saying that in such cases the whole arterial system is diseased ; and not straightforward, because he wrote of Hunter's first operation, " I once saw an attempt of this kind, in which I shall only remark that the patient died ; and I do believe that the embarrassments which occurred, as well as the event of the operation, will deter the gentleman who performed it from making a second attempt in a similar case." But the patient died fifteen months after the operation, neither of it nor of the aneurysm.

The vacancies caused by the retirement of Cæsar Hawkins and of Bromfield were filled by two of Cæsar Hawkins' family : Charles, his son, and George, his nephew ; but the latter ceased to hold office in 1783. His place was taken by William Walker ; so that the surgical staff was now Gunning, Hunter, Charles Hawkins, and Walker. This year a proposal was made by Hunter, or at least supported by him, that a medical school should be created, after the model of the Guy's Hospital school, and that each surgeon should give six lectures on surgery. " It was not approved by Hunter's colleagues, and reasons were assigned by them for the rejection of it, which for the most part seem to have been dictated by a feeling of opposition to Hunter, and cannot be said to be based on any valid ground of argument." (Page.)

In 1787, application was made by Gunning and Hunter, that each of them might have an assistant surgeon :—

JOHN HUNTER

"Mr. Gunning and Mr. Hunter present their compliments to the gentlemen of the weekly board, and beg the favour of them to summon a Special General Court for the purpose of electing two assistants, a favour which has been formerly shown to Mr. Middleton, Mr. Hawkins, and Mr. Bromfield, in consideration of their many years' services to the hospital.

"The persons whom they beg leave to recommend to this situation are Mr. Keate, Surgeon in ordinary to His Royal Highness the Prince of Wales, and Mr. Home, who has been bred up under Mr. Hunter.

"They flatter themselves the propriety of their recommendation will render this indulgence the less exceptionable."

Thomas Keate and Everard Home were duly appointed assistant-surgeons; and the two surgeons assured the Board that they had no intention of giving up their own attendance at the hospital on all necessary occasions.

Next year, 1788, Hunter had so exasperated his surgical colleagues by insisting that they ought to do more for the pupils, that in September they addressed a memorial to the Governors, in which they said:—

"On the subject of lectures—to take leave of this point which has been so much insisted on—we must declare our joint opinions, and they are incontrovertible. If they had been practical and contained principles and rules founded upon judgment and experience, with a regard to the authority of others as well as their own, they would have been highly useful ; if, on the contrary, they had leaned to physiology and experiment, with a contempt for all other opinions but their own, they would have been pernicious. The good therefore arising from lectures, unless under certain conditions, must be at least problematical."

Thus, in 1788, there was already war between Hunter and his colleagues : they refused to work with him for the school, and addressed the Board with a memorial against him. He was not likely to make peace with men who used these weapons ; and in 1792 came a crisis which forbade all hope of peace. Early that year Charles Hawkins resigned, and Keate and Everard Home both became candidates for the vacant office of surgeon to the hospital. Home was supported by Hunter, and by Dr. Matthew Baillie, Hunter's nephew ; against them were all the rest of the staff, in support of Keate. "The contest was perhaps the warmest in the annals of hospital electioneering, and several of the Royal Dukes attended in person to vote for Mr. Keate, who was chosen by a majority of 134 against 102." (Ottley.)

Henceforth Hunter was in vehement opposition to all the other surgeons, and exposed himself to such provocation as must endanger his life. The quarrels of the surgical staff were all over London, for they were all of them men of high position in the profession. Jesse Foot's account of them is to be noted here, allowance being made for his hatred of Hunter :—

"John Hunter could never separate the loss of Chelsea Hospital from the person of Keate; nor would he permit himself to reflect that he had not the influence for obtaining what Keate had, and what, if Keate had not obtained, another might; and that whoever had succeeded to it would have been equally obnoxious to him, as long as such a malignant impression remained upon his distempered mind. With Gunning he had been acquainted more than thirty years; and notwithstanding he had made man the study of his life, the book of nature must have been blotted on that page which could have informed him that Gunning would never tamely submit to a personal insult from any one. To Walker he had been well known only a few years less; and he must have evinced a superiority in the art of tormenting, above all competition, when he urged his good nature to enmity. He certainly misjudged his own power when he broke a lance with Keate in trying to keep him out of St. George's Hospital. Besides the mortification he experienced from finding that Keate's influence was superior to his own, he brought another proof, fatal to his ambition, to the test—that in the contest almost the whole of the respectable part of the faculty, in Westminster, were against him."

With 1793, the year of Hunter's death, his fight against his colleagues became less honourable to him.

ST. GEORGE'S HOSPITAL

He declared that the entrance-fees of the pupils should no longer be divided equally among the surgeons : he would keep for himself the fees of those pupils who entered under him. How far he wanted the money, or thought by this plan to force his colleagues to do more teaching, or was only moved by dislike of them, we do not know. Against this extraordinary policy the three surgeons said they would appeal to the Governors. Then Hunter wrote to them :—

GENTLEMEN,—As the time approaches when you propose referring to the Governors of St. George's Hospital my determination respecting the money arising from the surgeons' pupils, I beg leave to acquaint you that I entirely agree with you in the mode that you have proposed, a mode I did not myself adopt, as it took from you the power of acceding to my proposal, and made me appear to the Governors as an accuser. But when you bring it before them I shall meet it fairly and very willingly.

I am, Gentlemen,
Your most obedient Servant,
JOHN HUNTER.

LEICESTER SQUARE, *Feb.* 8, 1793.
Messrs. Gunning, Walker, and Keate.

A Special Court was summoned to meet in March. Before the meeting, Hunter sent to every subscriber a long printed letter, saying that all his attempts to improve the teaching of the hospital had been frustrated; therefore he had resolved not to encourage the idleness of his colleagues, and had given up trying, and the number of pupils had at once gone down: and the great majority had always entered under him, not under his colleagues, and each surgeon ought to get the profits that he deserved, neither more nor less:—

"When I solicited to be appointed one of the surgeons to St. George's Hospital, it was not with a view to augment my income, either immediately by the profits of the hospital, or in a secondary way by increasing my practice; but to acquire opportunities of extending my knowledge, that I might be more useful to mankind, not only by improving my private practice, but if I should be enabled to make discoveries even in the art itself. I had a view also to the instruction of those who were studying under me, particularly to that of the pupils of the hospital, whose improvement is one principal benefit accruing to the public from such instructions, and I have reason to believe that my intentions and endeavours in all these points have been attended with some success. . . . I conceived that the governors would wish that not only immediate relief should be given to the poor and distressed, but that the hospital should diffuse its influence to mankind in general; and by these means, even to themselves. I concluded that to render the hospital of such universal use would be agreeable to the feelings of the governors of this charity, and probably considered by

ST. GEORGE'S HOSPITAL

them as the most important service. I conceived to give an hospital a reputation for improvement it was to invite the philosopher as well as the charitable to contribute to its support. Other hospitals were beginning to participate in the improving spirit of the times, more especially those into which the younger surgeons had been elected. They united their powers and had lectures given to their pupils not only in surgery, but in every branch of the healing art. Mr. Pott, though one of the senior surgeons in London, gave lectures to the pupils of St. Bartholomew's Hospital, which lectures became the basis of his works on the operations in surgery, and do credit to the governors of that charity for their choice of one so able to instruct. . . . Finding the pupils of St. George's Hospital fewer than they had formerly been, I imputed it to the want of that increasing attention which the surrounding improvements in the art required, for one part should keep pace with the other. My practice in the hospital soon convinced me that this observation was just, and having been long in the habit of improving myself along with others, it had become in a manner natural to me. . . .

"When I mentioned what the medical gentlemen of other hospitals did, and what I thought we should do, one gentleman said 'He did not choose to lose any reputation he might have in surgery by giving lectures,' which at least was modest. Talking of the improvement of the art, one of the surgeons confessed 'He did not see where the art could be improved.' The natural conclusion from this declaration was that such a man would never improve it; but the answer then made was, 'To see where anything could be improved might be considered as going almost halfway towards the improvement itself; and that Lord Bacon was the cause of all the advances in philosophy since his day, by seeing and pointing out where and how they might be made.'" . . .

Hunter goes on to say, of Keate's election as surgeon the year before :—"In this, as in most other public contests, the mind, inflamed by opposition, lost sight of the great object, by which means private friendships and connections had more weight than public utility, to which object the governors will not on the present occasion confine themselves. My motive was in the first place to serve the hospital, and in the second to diffuse the knowledge of the art, that all might be partakers of it; this, indeed, is the highest office in which a surgeon can be employed; for when considered as a man qualified only to dress a sore or perform a common operation, and perhaps not all of those that may be reckoned common, he cannot be esteemed an ornament to his profession. . . . The governors will consider how far a numerous class of pupils increases the reputation of the hospital; they will consider whether those numbers do not produce the secondary good arising from an hospital, which is the effectual diffusion of knowledge, and, if so, whether every surgeon should not be in duty bound to contribute his share towards this good purpose. . . .

"I hope this Court will not consider this as similar to a contested election between two men. It is of general interest; it concerns no individual, or, if any, only four men who are servants of the hospital; and though in one point of view I may appear to stand single, yet I stand on equal ground with the governors of this charity, who formerly established the very law the advantages of which I have now illustrated. Indeed, from a consciousness of the disinterestedness of my motives, and a conviction of the clearness of the question in point of public utility, which I trust they cannot overlook and will not disregard, it would give me more pleasure to see the friends of the other gentlemen here to-day than my own. In whatever way it may be determined to me is personally immaterial; the good of mankind, the improvement of the healing art, and the character of the hospital, are the motives of my conduct, and according to which, whatever may be the decision of the present question, I shall continue to do my duty to the hospital as a charity, and confine myself to the laws of the institution.

JOHN HUNTER.

LEICESTER SQUARE, *February* 28, 1793.

Then came a counter-blast from the three surgeons. True, there had been more pupils since Hunter had joined the hospital; but that was because of the wars, not because of him. True, there had been fewer pupils of late years; but other hospitals had started schools, and had drawn men away from St. George's. True, again, Hunter had more pupils than any of them; thanks to his connection with his brother's school in Great Windmill Street, and to his having military appointments to give away. They had done their work on the old lines; and it was not their fault if the young men went straying after physiology. They had opposed, in 1783, the giving of lectures: for there were three reasons against the scheme: (1) Lectures were not so useful as bedside teaching. (2) The lectures would be copied out and passed from hand to hand till they were everybody's property. (3) They would involve raising the entrance fees. Finally, if the pupils' fees were not divided among all the surgeons, then each pupil would see the work of one surgeon only, and the other three would do nothing for him.

The Special Court decided against Hunter. The entrance fees were to be equally divided. They further appointed a Committee to draw up rules for the admission and teaching of the pupils. Hereupon the three surgeons, without consulting Hunter, submitted to the Committee the following proposals. I give their letter at length, for the account that it contains of the surgical work of the hospital a hundred years ago :—

ST. GEORGE'S HOSPITAL

To the Committee at St. George's Hospital, appointed to examine the Laws relative to the Surgeons' Pupils, and to consider of the best methods of Improving their Education.

We, the undersigned, beg leave to make the following statement.

GENTLEMEN,

In moving for the present Committee we have two principal objects in view. The one is a restoration, as far as may be useful, of the antient discipline of the hospital respecting the surgeons and their pupils. The other is the introducing of such improvements for the purposes of instruction as are now, and have been for some time, adopted by hospitals of the first consequence. In the first place, therefore, as far as relates to themselves, they leave all such rules now existing, as are not become useless, *in statu quo*, but they are of opinion that it will be indispensably necessary for the four surgeons belonging to this hospital to visit all their patients twice a week, and to be present themselves at the dressing of them once, and to visit them on the remaining days of the week as often as may be necessary. They further think that they ought to meet every Friday in consultation without being summoned, and that any defaulter ought to be reported to the weekly board, and from thence referred to a general court, to be dealt with for such breach of duty as they shall see proper; the surgeons being perfectly satisfy'd that such a regulation is of the utmost importance for the good of the patients; and that the close attendance of the surgeons is indispensably necessary for the instruction of the pupils.

They wish also to have it resolved that no operation shall be performed but on extraordinary occasions, such as accidents, except on Mondays, Wednesdays, and Fridays, and that no summonses shall be sent out for that purpose. If any particular day is assigned for operations, as was formerly the practice, and is common now at other hospitals, the pupils are ready to attend on that day, but frequently discontinue or relax in their attendance on other days, and by that means are ignorant of many essential parts of that knowledge which can only be attained by a general attendance at an hospital. The pupils, therefore, should be taught that a sufficient knowledge of their profession cannot be acquired without a constant and daily attendance.

They hope the Committee will determine that there shall be two hours allowed for the chirurgical business of the hospital—from eleven o'clock till one—that the dressings shall be finished at a quarter after twelve, and that the time that remains shall be apportioned for extra business if there be any. By extra business is understood the attendance on the board, on operations, on consultations, and the examination of morbid bodies. They hope your Committee will direct that every surgeon shall examine, or cause to be examined by some other surgeon of the hospital, the morbid bodies in the presence of all their pupils, of

ST. GEORGE'S HOSPITAL

which notice shall be given on the preceding day unless there be a convenient time for the examination on the immediate day.

We are further of opinion that it will be proper for the Committee to resolve that an operation shall be performed on a dead body, attended with explanations, or a lecture be given on some of the principal parts of surgery, once a week, by one of the surgeons in rotation, during nine months of the year, and that *gratis*.

We recommend it further to the Committee, and propose it as an object of great utility, that they will direct that a book shall be kept by the house surgeon for the instruction of the pupils, wherein shall be entered the material cases, the admission of the patients, their treatment, and the event, together with the appearances on the examination of morbid bodies; that each pupil shall be allowed to take a copy of such entries at his leisure, and that Saturday in every week shall be set apart for that purpose.

In the second place, respecting the pupils, we wish that the Committee will resolve that to whomsoever the pupils pay the fee for attending this hospital, they shall bring certificates of their having been bred up to the profession, and of their good behaviour, as till of late has been customary there, and in some degree the practice at other hospitals; that they shall be entered at the weekly board by the junior surgeon, and that they be told that if they do not comply with the rules enjoined them, they may be reprimanded or expelled without returning any part of the fee paid down on entering. This rule ought to be strictly enforced, as it will cause good behaviour and subordination, and prevent ignorant and improper persons from intruding themselves into the profession.

We wish the Committee further to resolve that no pupil shall be entered for a less period than one year, or half a year, except during the time of war, when it may be necessary for young men destined for the sea or land service to get what knowledge they can, and such as the usual short notice will admit of. The last regulation, allowing the attendance of quarterly pupils, is of a private nature, and was never sanctioned by the board; it was first adopted in the time of war, and afterwards improperly continued, as it must be readily admitted that no material knowledge can be acquired within so short a space as that of a quarter of a year.

We are further of opinion that it will be proper for the Committee to resolve that every pupil shall be considered as receiving his instructions from the hospital at large, and consequently under the care of all the surgeons alike. That no pupil shall be allowed to dress the patients unless he has attended the hospital three months. That no pupil shall be capable of being chosen the house surgeon unless he has been a dresser for six months, and unless he is at the time of his election a yearly pupil of the hospital. That they dress in turn, and according to seniority. That their time of attending the hospital shall be every day from

ST. GEORGE'S HOSPITAL

the hour of eleven till one. That they shall be sent for in case of operations arising from accidents if they lodge within a reasonable distance. That no leave of absence shall be granted for a longer time than three months. That no pupil shall be allowed a certificate but in cases of strict attendance, and that it be apply'd for at the time of his leaving the hospital, unless he is absent on foreign service.

Our first object, the restoration and the melioration of the antient discipline of this hospital, being thus effected and straightened by the addition of the rules above mentioned, we will pass to our second object, and consider the improved state of other hospitals, and compare it with our own as far as relates to lectures and the establishment of medical schools, which are now so universally prevalent, and which have been allowed and provided for by the governors of other hospitals. In St. Thomas's and Guy's Hospitals, which are contiguous and united for common instruction and emolument, in St. Bartholomew's and in the London, the whole course of lectures for the improvement of pupils in chirurgical and medical knowledge, except the lectures in Midwifery at St. Thomas's, which are not yet brought home, are concentrated within the verge of the respective hospitals. They consist of Midwifery, Surgery, the Materia Medica, with the Practice of Physick, of Chymistry, and Anatomy. The fees arising from an attendance on either or all are appropriated to the different professors only (for none are read gratis) and are not shared by either the physicians or surgeons belonging to the hospitals.

The obvious advantage of such an arrangement is this, that the pupils designed for either profession have not only set before them a complete class of such lectures as they may choose to attend, but do not lose a very considerable portion of their time in the morning now appropriated to these pursuits, by running about perhaps at great distances from one lecture to another and to the hospital; always inconvenient, and sometimes impracticable. They have formed there a complete school, at each of which, with respect to the arrangement of time, it is a principal object amongst the surgeons, however the lecturers may divide theirs, that there shall be an allowance of two hours, from eleven to one, for the attendance of pupils at either hospital.

The number of patients at St. Thomas's and Guy's is about 700, at St. Bartholomew's about 400, at the London Hospital about 140.

As to fees for attendance—those for apprentices excepted, which are always private, as are those for the dressers, indeed, at the hospitals of St. Thomas's and Guy's and St. Bartholomew's, and belong to their respective surgeons—for dressing they pay £50 each, or guineas, for one year; for general attendance only, £25; for the half-year, £18. The fees for the pupils at large are divided among the surgeons alike.

ST. GEORGE'S HOSPITAL

They admit no quarterly pupils. At the London Hospital, where the patients are not so numerous as at our own, and the discipline the same with respect to pupils and dressers, they are higher by one-third in their price, and take quarterly pupils as we do. They receive thirty guineas for the year, eighteen guineas for the half, and twelve guineas for the quarterly, compensating, we suppose, for the inferior number of their patients by the regularity and instruction of their school.

With respect to our own hospital, the price for the yearly pupil is twenty guineas; for the half-yearly, fifteen guineas; for the quarterly, ten guineas. We are then upon the lowest footing of all with respect to price.

As to the attendance of our pupils on lectures, they have to go for their Anatomy to Windmill Street; for their Midwifery to Queen Street, Golden Square; for their Chymistry, Materia Medica, and Practice of Physick to Leicester-fields. There are other lectures likewise, we believe, but all a considerable distance from the hospital, and there is probably an hour and a half lost every morning in the course of this diffused attendance; and it is but seldom that three-quarters of an hour or an hour, and this at an average not above three or four times a week (the dressers excepted), can be allotted for their chirurgical attendance at the hospital—a space too short for acquiring this kind of knowledge, or even of any knowledge at all. The

JOHN HUNTER

barely seeing operations in a theatre, at a distance, half of which perhaps they will never be called upon to perform, is but a trifling advantage, but this in general is what they content themselves with; and hence it is that it is possible, and even probable, that they may pass through an hospital after a year of such attendance without acquiring any substantial knowledge at all. The mode of attending so many lectures at a time, and those crowded and compressed within the morning, cannot add much to this superficial knowledge. However, they are not under the necessity of attending them all, and it must be confessed that there is an advantage in having them all to choose from.

A great part of this inconvenience you may remedy, by giving them the time they so much want; it will be giving them in reality a three years' attendance for one. To finish, therefore, this detail: it is obvious from the above statement, and comparing the course of improvement, adopted by the different hospitals, with our own, which has been hitherto chirurgical, and was at its first institution excellent, but is now become inferior from the causes we have explained, that we cannot stand our ground, and much less advance, unless the governors will give us leave to adopt the mode of discipline and instruction used by other hospitals, wherever it shall be found superior to our own, and unless they give us leave likewise to bring home the different professors to the hospital as soon as they can be engaged ; and, in one word, to permit us to act upon that extended plan which has been so wisely established and so fortunately executed by others.

May ye 27*th*, 1793.   J. GUNNING.
WM. WALKER.
T. KEATE.

Next month Hunter wrote to the Governors :—

To the Chairman of the Special General Court, St. George's Hospital.

MR. CHAIRMAN,—Having on most occasions been desirous of promoting the surgical education at the hospital, my name not appearing to the present proposals may give an idea of my being less zealous than usual on that subject. I beg leave to say that this is not the case ; but not having been consulted by my colleagues who drew them up, nor the Committee by which they were approved, my assistance has been supposed unnecessary.

They certainly appear to me in many respects very incompleat, and in some altogether unpracticable ; but if they meet with the approbation of the governors, it is my business, as a servant of the charity, to do the duty of my situation.

Your most obedient servant,
JOHN HUNTER.
LEICESTER SQUARE, *June* 14, 1793.

JOHN HUNTER

The proposals of the three surgeons were accepted; now there was at least a possibility of peace. But Hunter could not forego his distinctive position as the surgeon who had most pupils, who was the great central figure of the hospital. That autumn, two young men came to be admitted under him, without certificates that they had been "bred up to the profession," and he promised that he would nevertheless ask the Board to let them enter; they must draw up a statement of their case, and he would lay it before the Board, at their meeting on Wednesday, October 16th.

On the Sunday before the Wednesday, he had a long talk with Mr. Adams about his own case.

On the Wednesday morning, he saw one of his friends who called at his house; he told him what was to happen at the meeting, and said that he was afraid there would be a dispute, and was sure it would be the death of him. He went into the work-rooms, and told his resident pupils some droll stories how children counterfeit disease. He left his house, to pay a visit before he drove to the hospital; he was in good spirits, whistling a Scotch air as he went out. He had forgotten his visiting list; William Clift took it after him to York Street, St. James's, the first place on the list. Hunter came out of the house, took the list, and in an animated tone told the coachman to drive to the hospital. The meeting had already begun; he presented the memorial from the young men, and spoke on their behalf. One of his colleagues flatly contradicted something he had said. Then came the end. Angina seized him; he turned toward another room, to fight out his pain by himself, and Dr. Matthew Baillie followed him; he went a few steps, groaned and fell into Dr. Robertson's arms, and died.

To set the time of Hunter's death by the course of history, Clift wrote this title on his account-book :—

JOHN HUNTER, ESQ., F.R.S.,

Surgeon-General to the Army, and
Inspector-General of Hospitals;
Surgeon to St. George's Hospital;
Surgeon-Extraordinary to the King;
&c., &c., &c.,
DIED OCTOBER 16TH, 1793,
On the same day, and perhaps hour,
that the unfortunate Marie Antoinette
Queen of France was beheaded in
Paris.

W. CLIFT.

VIII

Ave Atque Vale

"Here was a Cæsar! When comes such another?"

IT is impossible to include in one view the multitudinous forms of Hunter's work; you cannot see the wood for the trees. He was anatomist, biologist, naturalist, physician, surgeon, and pathologist, all at once, and all in the highest. Nor is it possible to reproduce the lights and shadows of that aspect of his life which was not turned toward science. Yet an attempt must be made here to draw him as it were in outline.

The visible John Hunter was five feet two inches high, strongly built, and toward the end of his life somewhat corpulent; his shoulders were broad and high, his neck very short; he was "uncommonly strong and active, very compactly made, and capable of great bodily exertion." His hair was of a reddish or auburn tint, afterward grey, at last white; he wore it curled at the back, not tied; his eyes were light-coloured; he dressed plainly, and not always neatly—

AVE ATQUE VALE

in the Reynolds portrait, he has an old coat of crimson velvet, loosely buttoned. His attacks of angina had given him a sort of trick in breathing—" by the exertions which he constantly made, after the manner of a cough, he seemed as if he solicited to set the circulation of blood a-going."

Both Adams and Abernethy praise his pleasant way of talking. The former says: " Mr. Hunter's manners were extremely companionable. His wit, or more properly his archness, was always well directed, and the slowness of his articulation enabled him to point and correct it almost as soon as it was uttered." Abernethy says: "Mr. Hunter was a man of very considerable humour. His views of subjects in general were quick and peculiar, and when so disposed he could place them in very ludicrous points of view." Once Mrs. Hunter had to defend Sir William Blizard—Mr. Blizard he was then—from her husband's pleasantries. It was at a dinner party, and Hunter dared not drink the wine, and his guest would not :—

"'Come, fellow,' said he, in his usual blunt way, to Mr. Blizard, 'Why don't you drink your wine?' Mr. B. pleaded in excuse a whitlow, which caused him much pain. Hunter would not allow the validity of the plea, but continued to urge him and ridicule his excuse. 'Come, come, John,' said Mrs. Hunter, 'you will please to remember that you were delirious for two days when you had a boil on your finger some time ago.' This turned the laugh against Hunter, who now ceased from importuning his guest."

There is more humour in his vehement appeals to his friends for contributions towards his collection:—

"The late Dr. Clarke had a preparation on which he set a high value, and Hunter had often viewed it with longing eyes. 'Come, Doctor,' said he, 'I positively must have that preparation.' 'No, John Hunter,' was the reply, 'you positively shall not.' 'You will not give it to me, then?' 'No.' 'Will you sell it?' 'No.' 'Well, then, take care I don't meet you with it in some dark lane at night, for, if I do, I'll murder you to get it.'"

"He was not unfrequently obliged to borrow of his friends, when his own funds were at a low ebb, and the temptation was strong. 'Pray, George,' said he one day to Mr. Nicol the bookseller, 'have you got any money in your pocket?' Mr. N. replied in the affirmative. 'Have you got five guineas? because if you have, and will lend it to me, you shall go halves?' 'Halves in what?' inquired his friend. 'Why, halves in a magnificent tiger which is now dying in Castle Street.' Mr. Nicol lent the money, and Hunter got the tiger."

Next may come three stories how he treated young men who were or wished to be his pupils: quick to understand them, and not unwilling to answer a fool according to his folly:—

"He was one morning at breakfast, when a young

AVE ATQUE VALE

man, who was on intimate terms with him as a friend and pupil, mentioned, as if casually, that he had some thoughts of giving a course of lectures on comparative anatomy. Hunter looked up, and drily replied, 'Sir, that is a bold undertaking; I had thoughts once myself of doing the same thing, but the difficulties and necessary qualifications were so great that I did not think myself competent to the task; but you, I dare say, may feel yourself quite equal to it.'"

"On his arrival in London, Mr. Thomas, in company with Mr. Nicol, by whom he was to be introduced, called on Hunter; they found him dressing. 'Well, young gentleman,' said Hunter, when the first ceremonies of introduction were over, 'so you are come to town to be a surgeon. And how long do you intend to stay?' 'One year,' was the reply. 'Then,' said he, 'I'll tell you what, that won't do. I've been here a great many years, and have worked hard too, and yet I don't know the principles of the art.' After some further conversation, Mr. T. was directed to call again in an hour, which he did, and accompanied Hunter to the hospital, where he said to him, after the business was over, 'Come to me to-morrow morning, young gentleman, and I will put you further in the way of things; come early in the morning, as soon after four as you can.' It was summer; Mr. Thomas kept the appointment, and found Hunter, at that early hour, busily engaged in dissecting beetles."

JOHN HUNTER

"Sir Anthony Carlisle, whilst a pupil at the Westminster Hospital, was anxious to become personally acquainted with Hunter. He introduced himself by calling and requesting his acceptance of a very delicate and well-executed preparation of the internal ear. Hunter was highly delighted with it, detained him to breakfast, and in the course of conversation encouraged him by saying, 'Any man who will set about a business, and do it as you have done that ear, may do anything he pleases in London.' On finding that Mr. Carlisle had not yet attended his lectures—as a reason for which he assigned his not being sufficiently advanced in professional knowledge to profit by them—'That, Sir,' said Mr. Hunter, 'is very complimentary, but I will give you a perpetual ticket, and shall be glad to see you whenever you will call.'"

In consultation, he was deliberate and of many words; for often he must put forward views that were strange and hard to accept; he would start with relating a case in point, and go on to a long discourse. With his patients, he made no mystery of their cases; and enjoyed illustrating them from the natural history of lower forms of life :—

"When the Duke of Queensberry broke his tendo Achillis, he was immediately aware of what had happened, and pointed out to me the broken ends. He readily submitted to my reasoning, walked about the room, and found it impracticable to contract his gastrocnemius muscle. Some surgeons thought the tendon could not be broken, because he was walking about his room; but in such a case the patient has no more power to contract his gastrocnemius and soleus muscles than to jump over St. Paul's." (Lectures on Surgery.)

"A gentleman begged that I would do it (a small operation) for him before he went to Paris. I objected, telling him my reasons. He was pleased with them, and postponed the operation until his return; and fortunately for himself." (Lectures on Surgery.)

"Mrs. Nicol, who was a sister of Cruikshank, had lost five children, and was in the family way for the sixth (the present Mr. N.). Hunter, in passing one day, dropped in, and asked Mr. Nicol whether he intended to kill this, as he had killed all the rest of his children. Mr. N., who was a North-countryman, had on false principles endeavoured to inure his children to cold and rough usage. He demanded of Hunter what he meant. 'Why,' said Hunter, 'do you know what is the temperature of a hen with her callow brood? Because if you don't, I'll tell you.' He then proceeded to explain the necessity of warmth to young animals, and convinced Mr. Nicol of the propriety of changing his plan."

"A strong, ruddy-faced farmer had a disease which induced Mr. Hunter to enjoin a total abstinence from fermented liquors. 'Sir,' said the farmer, 'that is impossible, for I cannot relinquish my employment; and you know, sir, it is impossible to work without some support.' Mr. Hunter, perceiving that his patient was not likely to be readily convinced, enquired how many acres of land he cultivated, and what number of them was arable. He next asked, how many horses were kept upon the farm: and then boldly asserted that they were too few in number for the quantity of land. The farmer maintained that they were sufficient, but was at length brought to confess that they were worked hard. 'Allow me then,' said Mr. Hunter, 'to enquire what it is that you give *them* to drink.'"

Once only, so far as we know, was he rough or brutal toward his patients or their friends; he asked leave to make a *post-mortem* examination, and it was refused. Over this loss of precious knowledge, he forgot himself; Abernethy tells the story, as he heard it from an eye-witness:—

"When he became conscious that his óbject was unattainable, he was standing with his back to the fire, and he put his hands into his pockets. I saw by his countenance that a storm was brewing in his mind. He gravely and calmly addressed the master of the house in the following manner, 'Then, sir, you will not permit the examination to be made?' 'It is impossible,' was the reply. 'Then, sir,' said Mr. Hunter, 'I heartily hope that yourself and all your family, nay, all your friends, may die of the same

AVE ATQUE VALE

disease, and that no one may be able to afford any assistance;' and so saying he departed."

Faults of temper do not count heavily against a man afflicted with angina; and the stories of Hunter's want of self-control, his rage when he was crossed over some trifle, belong most of them to his later life. They are not worth re-telling here; sometimes his anger was so irrational and so soon past that it might be regarded rather as the effect than as the cause of the instability of his nervous system. For he knew that every time he lost his temper he stood to lose his life, and he had a steady hold over himself in everything else :—he abstained from wine at a time when wine was drunk like water, forced himself to give lectures and write books, made men work under him, took his place high in London society, and crowded every sort of hard work into a life that was full of pain.

There are many stories of his generosity;[1] how he remitted or returned his fees, and kept "the grandees" waiting, while he saw some patient to whom time was money. He was especially kind to poor artists and poor doctors; there was, for example, Mr. Lynn, who

---

[1] "In regard to fees, Hunter was extremely liberal. He used generally to reply, when asked to say what was due to him, 'Why, that you must determine yourself; you are the best judge of your own circumstances, and it is far from my wish to deprive you of the comforts of life.' He never allowed himself to accept any remuneration from non-beneficed clergymen, professional authors, or artists of any sort, and sometimes returned large fees when he found that the parties were in embarrassed circumstances" (Ottley).

became inoculated, at a *post-mortem* examination, with a grave contagious disease : [1]—

"When I was ill, he kindly and diligently attended me; nay, he brought those of his medical friends to visit me in whose judgment he placed most confidence. My illness however being tedious, I was at length obliged to go into the country for the recovery of my health. Mr. Hunter called on me before my departure, and said, 'I have been thinking that you might want a little money; if so, I can procure you £200; though in general I am the most unlikely person in this town to have money at command.' I thanked him, but told him I had been more provident than perhaps might have been expected, therefore I did not want money. On my return to town, and re-establishment in business, which did not take place for a considerable time, I took an opportunity of expressing to Mr. Hunter my continued sense of gratitude for his kindness in attending me, and for his offer of pecuniary assistance. 'Hah,' said he, 'I offer you money! that is droll indeed; for I am the last person in this town to have money at command. I have entirely forgotten it. But of this I am assured, that what I offered I meant to perform.'"

He found time for a pleasure now and again; he speaks of his club, of a few days in the country, of a

---

[1] William Lynn, born 1753. He assisted Hunter, for twelve years, in the work of the Museum : member of the Corporation of Surgeons, 1786 : surgeon to Westminster Hospital : President of the Royal College of Surgeons, 1825 : died January 24, 1837.

visit to the theatre to see Mrs. Siddons, and of going to see a mesmerist, who tried in vain to mesmerise him; and he gave dinners, and went to them; but in the later years of his life he could not stand what is called "sustained conversation." He hated ceremonies; when he had to attend the public funeral of Reynolds, he wished Reynolds and his friends would go to the devil; and he was present at one meeting only of the Court of Assistants of the Corporation of Surgeons. But where he could teach or learn, as at the Societies, he was zealous in attendance; and was called the Cerberus of the Royal Society. Perhaps it was this dislike of public formalities that made him give evidence so badly in the sensational trial of Captain Donellan, in March, 1781, for the murder of his brother-in-law, Sir Theodosius Boughton, by giving him laurel-water in his drink; dislike of formalities, and indignation that the evidence against Donellan was supported by experiments made without experience.[1] He would say nothing certain, was taken to task, severely cross-examined, bullied by Mr. Justice Buller; yet he had administered laurel-water to himself, to see how it acted. He often experimented on himself; so early as 1765, he inoculated himself, by a most unhappy mistake in the experiment, with

[1] "A poor devil was lately hanged at Warwick upon no other testimony than that of physical men whose first experiments were made on this occasion." (Lectures on Surgery, "Of Humours.") Mr. Shelton, the Coroner for London, afterward said that Hunter had been treated very badly at the trial.

the wrong virus, and suffered two years from the effects of it—an error which served only to support false notions in pathology.

He loved his home-life, and often said that if he had been allowed to bespeak a pair of children, they should have been those with which Providence had favoured him. He liked his friends to call him by his Christian name; and the doorplate in Leicester Square bore only his name, without Mr. before it or letters after it. In politics, he was a Tory, and would say that he wished all the rascals who were dissatisfied with their country would be good enough to leave it: and near the end of his life, in reply to a request that some foreign gentleman might be allowed to go over his Museum, he wrote, "If your friend is in London in October (and not a Democrate) he is welcomb to see it; but I would rather see it in a blaze, like the Bastile, than show it to a Democrate, let his country be what it may." In religion, he was silent alike in his letters, his lectures, and his books: and that at a time when silence in such lectures and books was the exception rather than the rule. When he was dead, a war arose over his belief regarding life, Lawrence against Abernethy, each with their followers; the same warfare that was roused over Darwin's work. There is in Hunter's writings a very slight preponderance of the transcendental interpretation of life as against the materialist; and here and there phrases occur which are irreconcileable with the strict logic of materialism.

AVE ATQUE VALE

But he had neither the education nor the temperament for philosophy; and he used a sort of psychological language that had not any relation to it. "Of all things on the face of the earth, definitions are the most cursed; for if you make a definition, you may bring together under it a thousand things that have not the least connection with it." (Lectures on Surgery.)

In the British Museum there is a copy of the auctioneer's catalogue of his books, which were sold on Feb. 1, 1794; some 1300 or 1400 volumes, in 171 lots; but we do not know which were his own, and which belonged to Mrs. Hunter. Beside surgical and scientific works, there was a good store of classics; some perhaps had been bought by the yard—a French History of England in 28 volumes, Shakespeare in 20, Pope in 20, Swift in 17; Chaucer, Rabelais, Ben Jonson, Bacon, all in many volumes. But there was another Shakespeare, in 8 volumes, and an Index, and a Concordance; probably he read Shakespeare; and he quotes Swift in his Lectures. There were several Bibles, and Cruden's Concordance; he may have read or learned his French and Spanish in the Bible, for there were copies of it in both languages, and more than twenty lexicons and dictionaries, English, French, Spanish, and Italian. Not a word of German. The number of Spanish books was considerable—Don Quixote in French, and in Italian, and in several Spanish editions; and there was a good quantity of

JOHN HUNTER

French classics. It is all guess-work; the books may have been used only by Mrs. Hunter and the children and the elocution-master. But the catalogue does suggest that Hunter kept up the French and Spanish that he learned at Belleisle and in the Peninsula.

Here and there in his Lectures he lets us see something of his character and his method of work. In illustration of his unwearied patience in thinking out a case—his habit of saying, "I cannot tell at present what to recommend; I must think of it"—these two remarks are worthy of note:—

"After about an hour's conversation with the patient, I made out a few simple facts."

"I called with a friend to pass a day or two in the country. The lady of the house had had her knee fractured. . . . She recovered from the accident, but was totally unable to use the limb. . . . Having spent a whole night in considering the probable cause of her loss of power, it appeared to me," &c.

His distrust of rapid thinking, his hatred of work published in a hurry, come again and again into the Lectures :—

"It is surprising to see how a young man, if he catches an idea which has any novelty, will write away on it and tell you wonders."

"Although the theory (of the cure of hydrocele) is very simple, yet no disease affecting the human body, and requiring an operation for its cure, has called forth the opinions and pens of surgeons so much as this

AVE ATQUE VALE

disease. The reason of this is easily accounted for ; for they have gone so far as to find out that every mode of operating but their own has failed, but have not noticed the cause of failure. It was enough for them that they could condemn. They rested contented with having recommended a method which was to them infallible ; nor did the condemnation of this favourite method of theirs by others rouse them into an enquiry as to the cause of its failure."

Therefore he published nothing, save a few short notes added to the writings of other men, till he was forty-three years old ; and his indifference to books, which has been somewhat exaggerated, was mostly because books hindered his pupils from observing and thinking for themselves. When Mr. Physick brought his son as a new pupil, and asked what books he should read, Hunter said, "Sir, follow me ; I will show you the books your son has to study " ; took him into the dissecting-room, and showed him the bodies ; "these are the books your son will learn under my direction, the others are fit for very little."

He is like Vesalius ; he made his name immortal by the labour of his own hands outside the sphere of surgery. Apart from all his hospital and private practice, and all his writing and lecturing, the actual manual work that he accomplished in dissections and *post-mortem* examinations is past all telling. Twelve years before he died, at Captain Donellan's trial, he was asked, "You have been long in the habit of dissecting human subjects; I presume you have dissected more than any man in Europe?" and he answered, "I have dissected some thousands during these thirty-three years." His dissections of animals must also be reckoned in thousands. Literary work was uncongenial to him, and against the grain; he took no pleasure in style and no pains over spelling, submitted his writings to the correction of his friends, adopted at their suggestion Greek words,[1] and that most foolish phrase "materia vitæ diffusa." But in anatomy and experiment he had the strength and patience of ten; and Clift often saw him, in his old age, standing like a statue for hours over some delicate bit of dissection.

The whole output of his working life is fourfold—literary, surgical, anatomical, physiological and experimental; but the multiplication together of these factors does not give the whole result of his work. He brought surgery into closer touch with science. Contrast him with Ambroise Paré, a surgeon in some ways like him, shrewd, observant, ahead of his age; the achievements of Paré, side by side with those of Hunter, are like child's play in comparison with the serious affairs of men; Paré advanced the art of surgery, but Hunter taught the science of it.

[1] "Jesse Foot accuses me of not understanding the dead languages; but I could teach him that on the dead body which he never knew in any language, dead or living."

IX

AFTER HUNTER

THE body of John Hunter was taken in a sedan-chair from the hospital to Leicester Square, followed by his colleagues. He had said, more than once, that he should wish his body to be examined, and this was done; the funeral was attended by those only who were in close friendship with him. He was buried in the vaults of St. Martin's-in-the-Fields. His widow could not afford the fees for his burial in Westminster Abbey; and it was against the rules that she should put a monument to him in St. Martin's church. In 1859, when the coffins in the vaults were moved for re-interment, Frank Buckland undertook to find Hunter's body. He began on January 26th, and searched for sixteen days, by which time he had viewed three thousand and sixty coffins; then he found it, when only three still remained for him to examine. On March 28, 1859, Hunter was buried with great honour in the North aisle of the

Abbey. There is a window to his memory in the church of St. Mary Abbott's, Kensington.

By his will, made July 11, 1793, he appointed Matthew Baillie and Everard Home executors. Long Calderwood he left to his son; Earl's Court House was to be sold; his collection was to be offered to the Government in one lot, then to any Foreign Government, then sold by auction in one lot.

" And I hereby direct that all my just debts be paid by and out of the monies to arise by sale of my real estate so directed to be sold as aforesaid; and out of the rents and profits thereof until such sale shall be had, and also by and out of the monies to arise by sale of my Natural History, and also by and out of my other personal estate. And I give and bequeath the residue and surplus of all such monies, and all other my personal estate, unto Ann, my dear and esteemed wife; John, my son; and Agnes, my only daughter; share and share alike; provided that, in case of the death of my son before he attains twenty-one, or of my daughter before she attains twenty-one, or marriage, then it is my will and intent that the capital of the share or part of such of them so dying, shall go and be paid to the survivor of them. And I do hereby nominate and appoint my said wife, and also the said Matthew Baillie and Everard Home, Guardians to my two children until they shall severally attain twenty-one years of age; and also Executors of this my will."

AFTER HUNTER

Long Calderwood had been left by William Hunter, in 1783, to his nephew, Dr. Matthew Baillie, who was then twenty-two years old. He had been educated first at the grammar school at Hamilton, where his father was minister, then at Glasgow College, then at Oxford.[1] During the vacations (his father died in 1778), he lived in William Hunter's house in Great Windmill Street, working and demonstrating for him, and at last taking the place of a son to him. The praise of Matthew Baillie cannot be set down here, nor what he did for medicine; we are concerned only with one of

---

[1] I.

From Thomas Reid to William Hunter.

GLASGOW COLLEGE, *May* 6, 1778.

DEAR SIR,—I cannot help condoling with you on the loss of our worthy Friend, Dr. Baillie (Matthew's father). The Family deserve great sympathy. Mrs. Baillie is one of the best of women, and the children all very hopefull. Matthew has all along given uncommon application to his Studies. I hope he will have the first Baliol exhibition that falls which is expected very soon . . .

II.

From Archbishop Cornwallis to William Hunter.

LAMBETH HOUSE, *March* 29, 1780.

SIR,—I would not trouble you with an answer to your letter till I could give you a positive one. I have now the pleasure to inform you that I have been able to comply with your request, and have concurred with the Bishop (of Rochester) in appointing Mr. Baillie to the Exhibition at Balliol College. I am sorry I was not at home when you did me the favour to call.

I am, Sir, your most humble Servant

FRED. CANT.

his many acts of generosity. Long Calderwood had belonged to William Hunter unconditionally; he had bought back much of the land that his father had sold; and he was free to leave the estate to whomever he chose. But Matthew Baillie, though in 1783 he was poor, and not even within sight of success, insisted that John Hunter should have the estate. "Dr. Baillie conveyed these lands to Mr. John Hunter, because he thought he had a better natural claim to them than himself. Dr. Baillie's conveyance to Mr. John Hunter is dated October, 1784. Mr. John Hunter, in taking up the estate, preferred doing it in the line of succession, which it was in his power to do; for having got the conveyance from Dr. Baillie, no person had any right to oppose him." (Adams).[1]

It is not likely that John Hunter in the later years of his life found time to visit Long Calderwood; but one of the last letters that he wrote was concerned with

---

[1] *From Matthew Baillie to Robert Barclay, Esq.*

... " With regard to the transferring of the estate, I can have no objection to any consultation, but the *names* must be *conceal'd*, and no circumstance brought forwards which may tend to discover the parties engag'd in the transaction. The more every matter of this kind can be done with secrecy, it is the better. I have never ventured more than once to talk of it myself to J. Hunter. He refus'd the offer, but not with any decided tone. I do not mean to talk of it again to him untill I have the deeds in my pocket ready to give him. This is a matter in which I am very much interested, and I think I shall nearly feel as much satisfaction in delivering over the deeds to J. Hunter as if a sum of the same value was to be given to myself."

the management of it. His son died and left no children, and it came to Matthew Baillie's son, Mr. William Hunter Baillie, and after his death to Miss Baillie, his daughter, the present owner.

Earl's Court House had a very different fate. Hunter had added wings to the house, and stables, and farm buildings, and conservatories; the gardens were of considerable extent, and well planted with trees. The Duke of Richmond had it for a time, then (1811) the Earl of Albemarle; the little Princess Charlotte used the Lions' Den as an excellent resort for hide and seek.[1] Later the Den became a cow-stall, and the house was taken as a private asylum. In February, 1886, there was a public auction, and the whole place was pulled down. The relics of John Hunter were not such as to command a high price; the copper where the Irish giant had been boiled was sold for thirty-six shillings; the panelled doors in the best bedroom fetched three pounds twelve shillings apiece. Earl's Court District Railway Station is opposite the site of the old house.

Photographs and drawings of Long Calderwood, Earl's Court House, and 28, Leicester Square, are in the Library of the Royal College of Surgeons.

The Leicester Square buildings are now in course of demolition (Sept., 1897) and will be gone in a few months. The pictures, engravings, and books were sold by Messrs. Christie and Manson, at a four days'

[1] Lady de Clifford, Lord Albemarle's mother, was her governess.

auction, in January and February, 1794. Among the pictures, 120 altogether, were works by Hogarth, Reynolds, Zoffany, and the big Zuccarelli cartoons, and a portrait of Harvey by Janssen; but the whole collection fetched only £800. The engravings, including many by Hogarth, Woollett, and Sharp, were sold for £140; the books for £160. Later, in July, there was a sale of the curios—armour, weapons, the big turning-lathe, and so forth; these went for £200. The whole sum raised by the sale was about £1,500.

The museum also must be sold; but in 1794 the Government was not in the mood for spending money on anatomy. "What! Buy preparations!" said Mr. Pitt, "why, I have not money enough to purchase gunpowder." He gave a grant of money to Mrs. Hunter, for 1794 and 1795; but it was no time for applying Government funds to the advancement of science.

From Lord Auckland to Sir Joseph Banks.
Jan. 25, 1796.

. . . "Our late friend John Hunter left *nothing* for the support of his widow and children, after the payment of his debts, but his collection of anatomical preparations. From respect for his memory, and from regard for Mrs. Hunter, whose conduct in such a position has been highly becoming, I have concurred with the Chief Baron during two years in obtaining for her, through Mr. Pitt, the aid of His Majesty's

AFTER HUNTER

bounty ; and I have been of some use to her in other respects. But the Act of Parliament does not allow the King's bounty to be given a third year. In the meantime the trustees of the collection (Mr. Home and Dr. Baillie) have not been able to induce the House of Commons to purchase it, or even to consider the subject. In truth, the agitation of their minds amidst the great scenes which are going forward, as well as a general impression that all avoidable expenses, not essential to the purposes of the war, should be postponed, have combined to make it difficult to recommend the purchase to the public. The delay is most distressing to the family, who have no other resource ; the mere expense of keeping the collection is an overwhelming weight to those who have nothing.

"I do not pretend to be able to form any adequate idea of the value and importance of the collection to science ; it is quite out of my line of observation. But I have always understood that your scientific leaders concur in thinking it highly curious, and well calculated to do service in the school both of medical and of natural philosophy in general.

"I trust that as the worthy President of the Royal Society, as an old and respected friend of a distinguished person whose family is left destitute, and, in short, as a man of science and of benevolence, you will turn this subject in your thoughts. If the purchase could be properly and effectually recommended, with the King's approbation, to the House of Commons and to the Minister at the head of the Treasury, it would be the best result."

From Sir Joseph Banks to Lord Auckland.

"MY DEAR LORD,—Had I thought my friend John Hunter's collection an object of importance to the general study of natural history, or indeed to any branch of science except to that of medicine, I hope that two years would not have elapsed without my taking an active part in recommending to the public the measure of purchasing it. I was consulted in the first instance by the gentlemen concerned, who, if I rightly understood them, agreed with me in thinking that the history of diseases was the only interesting and valuable part, and the natural history was not of consequence sufficient to be brought forward as an object of public purchase.

"Concluding that the history of diseases arranged itself naturally under the protection of the College of Surgeons, and knowing that the corporate mansion of that learned body was roomy enough to receive the collection; being well aware that matters of abstract medicine did not come within the province of the Royal Society, knowing that the apartments of that body are scarce able to contain the property they already possess, and thinking the museum, to which, from the nature of its institution, students could not have a convenient access, an improper deposit, I declined, with the full approbation as I thought of the parties concerned, taking any lead in the matter."

AFTER HUNTER

Still, Sir Joseph Banks would gladly help Lord Auckland so far as he could. The House of Commons appointed a Committee to take evidence as to the value of the collection, and the cost of its maintenance; and on June 13, 1799, the sum of £15,000 was voted for its purchase. There was some idea that it should be transferred to the Royal College of Physicians, or to the British Museum; but the Corporation of Surgeons, by a unanimous vote taken on December 23, 1799, agreed to receive it under conditions fixed by the Government.

Till 1806, the collection remained in Leicester Square, guarded by William Clift; it was accessible to visitors, he says, but very few came. Of all the men whose lives came close to Hunter's life, the two most romantic figures are his brother Jamie, who died when Hunter was a boy, and Clift, who was a boy when Hunter died. He was born on Hunter's birthday, February 14, 1775, at Burcombe near Bodmin. He was brought up in poverty, went to school at Bodmin, had a taste for drawing, and used to adorn the kitchen floor with sketches in chalk. Mrs. Gilbert, of The Priory, Bodmin, who had been a schoolfellow of Mrs. Hunter,[1] took notice of him, and sent him up

---

[1] Mrs. Gilbert died in 1818, and left a legacy of £50 to Mr. Clift; Mrs. Hunter wrote of it to him; her letter is in the possession of the Royal College of Surgeons:—

Saturday, April 11, 1818.
LR. GROSVR. STR.

I have this day had a letter from Bodmin, announcing the death of my dearest and oldest friend; I know this news will grieve you, my good

JOHN HUNTER

to London to her old friend. Young Clift came to Leicester Square on February 14, 1792; again, John Hunter's birthday. Board and lodging were given to him in Castle Street, and he was set to write and to make drawings, to dissect, and to take part in the charge of the museum. For a year and eight months he saw and wondered at the incessant rush of work and fashion through the great house in Leicester Square; then came the end of it all, and he took up again with poverty, and lived, year after year, with an old housekeeper, in the dreary Castle Street house, on seven shillings a week; and at one time, from the war with France, a quartern loaf was two shillings. He kept things together, watched over the museum, had access to Hunter's manuscripts, and was without books of his own; therefore, he set himself to transcribe the manuscripts.[1]

The Government had given £15,000 for the collection on June 13, 1799; the Corporation of Surgeons had agreed, on December 23, to take charge of it. With the coming of the nineteenth century, the old order changed. In 1800, the surgeons, by a charter dated March 22, became the Royal College of Surgeons

Clift, but let it be some comfort to know, she did not suffer, but merely went to sleep without a groan, or even a sigh. . . .

[1] "After Mr. Hunter's death, till 1806, I had the key of the cases which contained the manuscripts, and was anxious to make myself acquainted with the nature of their contents, as they related chiefly to the preparations. I had also, I may say, no other books to read at that time; so I frequently availed myself of the opportunity to read them, and make extracts from them."

AFTER HUNTER

in London ; they gave up Surgeons' Hall, and took a house in Lincoln's Inn Fields, on the site of part of the present buildings. In 1806, they received from Parliament a grant of £15,000 to build a museum in Lincoln's Inn Fields ; three years later, a second grant of £12,500 ; and they spent, of their own money, more than £21,000. By the charter of 1800, they were empowered to examine candidates for the membership of the College ; and the examination-fees helped them to support this heavy expenditure of so many thousand pounds. Other charters were granted to them in 1821, 1843, and 1888 ; under the charter of 1843 they received the title of the Royal College of Surgeons of England, and the Fellowship was instituted.

The Museum and Library, begun in 1806 and finished in 1813, became in a few years overcrowded with preparations and books ; and in 1835-36 the whole building was reconstructed by Sir Charles Barry. In 1847, the College bought Mr. Copeland's premises in Portugal Street, and in 1852 built on them the Eastern Museum. In 1888, the premises were again enlarged ; two more museums were added, and the Conservator's house on the Eastern side of the building was pulled down, making room for the extension of the Library.

From 1793 to 1800, Clift was left to fight poverty in Castle Street, on seven shillings a week, all that

JOHN HUNTER

John Hunter's executors could afford, with permission to use enough spirits to keep the preparations from spoiling. When the Royal College of Surgeons came into existence, he was made Conservator of the collection (July, 1800) and received £100 a year; and seven members of the Council were appointed Curators, to write a catalogue, and to determine rules for the safe keeping of the specimens.

In 1806, the collection was removed from Castle Street to the house in Lincoln's Inn Fields. Here, says Clift, it was wholly inaccessible; "it was in store-rooms, in fact, in the dwelling-house, from the top to the bottom." When a half of the new museum was built, the preparations were moved into that half; and in 1813, when the museum was finished, they were at last properly arranged, and displayed to visitors; the chief of whom, that year, was Cuvier, who had thirty or forty drawings made for him.

John Hunter had passed his thirtieth year before he made a single preparation for himself; all that he made before that time were added to his brother's collection. He died when he was sixty-five, and his life was so full of other work—writing, lecturing, hospital and private practice, experiments on animals, duties administrative and social—and this work was so often stopped by sickness, that we should still praise his unwearied industry, though he had never put two specimens together. But he had dissected with his own hands, and had described—

AFTER HUNTER

Of Quadrumana	... ...	21 species
Carnivora ...	... ...	51 ,,
Rodentia ...	... ...	20 ,,
Edentata ...	... ...	5 ,,
Ruminantia	... ...	15 ,,
Pachydermata	... ...	10 ,,
Cetacea ...	... ...	6 ,,
Marsupiata...	... ...	10 ,,
Birds ...	... ...	84 ,,
Reptiles ...	... ...	25 ,,
Fishes ...	... ...	19 ,,
Insects ...	... ...	29 ,,
Other Invertebrata	...	20 ,,

315

"From the titles of his manuscripts, it appears that Hunter possessed, at the period of his decease, original records of the dissection of three hundred and fifteen different species of animals. In addition to these, Hunter's preparations testify that he had dissected twenty-three species of mammalia, sixteen species of birds, fourteen species of reptiles, forty species of fishes, forty-two different mollusca, and about sixty species of articulate and radiate animals; all species of animals of whose anatomy we have no evidence that he left written descriptions. So that by adding these undescribed dissections to those of which we derive the evidence from the list of the manuscripts, there is proof that Hunter anatomised at least five hundred different species of animals, *exclusive of repeated dissections of different individuals of the same species*, besides the dissection of plants to a considerable amount. With regard to the rarer and less known invertebrate animals, he was not content with merely recording their structure, and displaying its leading peculiarities in preparations; but he caused most elaborate and accurate drawings to be made from the recent dissections." (Owen.)

But these specimens illustrating comparative anatomy or physiology were but a small part of the collection. He added to them, by the work of his own hands, or by incessant expenditure of money, thousands of preparations in human anatomy, and in pathology; skulls of all nations, stuffed animals, fossils; two thousand stuffed animals, three thousand fossils. Prof. Charles Stewart and Mr. Timothy Holmes have estimated the sum of the whole collection at more than 13,000 specimens:—

Physiological preparations, in spirit	3,745
Osteological preparations … …	965
Dry preparations … … …	617
Zoological (stuffed animals) …	1,968
Fossils—	
Vertebrate … … …	1,215
Invertebrate … … …	2,202
Plants … … …	292

AFTER HUNTER

Pathological preparations, in spirit...	1,084
Dry preparations	625
Calculi	536
Malformations	218
Microscopic preparations	215
	13,682

Yet these figures represent but a part of his work. Over and above his endless toil for his collection, and all his other daily tasks for surgery, he was for ever making experiments. He studied the development of eggs, and pursued his studies for fifteen years; "surely one might suppose that this was the great work of his life; yet it seems to have been rather a casual by-the-way pursuit." For years he watched the habits of bees and wasps; "he says that in his experiments on bees he killed several hives and examined every single bee, to assure himself that no male was left after the fertilisation of the queen bee had been effected. Now the number of labourers in a hive amounts to at least 4,000, so that he must have examined twelve or fifteen thousand bees one by one, to determine this point alone." (Power, Hunterian Oration).

Finally, he recorded, with infinite patience, all that he did. At his death, he left an enormous quantity of manuscripts; and the strange story of these manuscripts must be told here, so far as possible, in Mr. Clift's own words.

JOHN HUNTER

"At Mr. Hunter's death, all his papers came into the possession of his executors, Dr. Baillie and Mr. Home. Mr. Home was the acting executor. The cabinets which contained these papers stood in Mr. Hunter's study, that he might have ready access to them in the evenings; and scarcely a single evening occurred, except Sundays, during my attendance on Mr. Hunter for the last twenty months of his life, in which something was not added to the contents of these volumes and papers. I wrote for him constantly during that period from seven o'clock till eleven p.m., and sometimes an hour or two later, as did also Mr. Haynes for a great part of that period. The greatest part of these papers were in the handwriting of Mr. Bell, who lived fourteen years in Mr. Hunter's house for the purpose of writing and making drawings.

"Mr. Hunter kept an account of the various animals that came under his inspection; and whenever he re-examined an animal, he overlooked his previous account, and corrected or added to it. Also an account of all remarkable and interesting cases that came under his observation, as well as others furnished by his friends.

"He generally wrote his first thoughts or memoranda on all subjects on the slips torn off from the ends and the blank pages and envelopes of letters. Thousands of these were copied by Haynes and myself into the different papers and volumes, being generally inserted and frequently pinned into the place where they were to be written in. He appeared to have no desire for preserving his own handwriting, as we always scored these slips across, and returned them to Mr. Hunter, who usually folded them up, and put them on the chimney-piece to light the candles with; and the rough or waste copies on all subjects, when copied out fair, were taken into his private dissecting room as waste paper to dissect upon.

"From the time of Mr. Hunter's death, and during nearly two years before that, while I was Mr. Hunter's apprentice, I had the entire charge of the collection. Shortly before the collection was transferred to the College of Surgeons (Dec., 1799), the manuscripts were taken by me in a cart to Sir Everard Home's house, by his order. He merely said that these papers, being a very large proportion of them loose fasciculi, were not fit for the public eye; and therefore he should take them into his keeping, for the purpose of using them in describing the collection."

For twenty-three years, from 1800 to 1823, the manuscripts remained in the possession of Sir Everard Home. The story how he then destroyed them was told by Mr. Clift in 1834, when he gave evidence before the Parliamentary Committee on Medical Education. An abstract of his evidence was published in the *Lancet*, July 11, 1835. Home had been urged by the trustees, again and again, to write the long-promised catalogue; he neither did this, nor allowed any one else to do it. In 1817 he rearranged the specimens, in 1818 he wrote a sort of general account of them; but the catalogue he never wrote. From the manuscripts, he conveyed what he wanted into the numerous papers that he read before the Royal Society, and into his Lectures on Comparative Anatomy; then, in July, 1823, having made this use of Hunter's writings as materials for his own advancement, he burned them.

From Mr. Clift's evidence before the Parliamentary Committee.

"*Q.* The Council have stated that in 1816 it was proposed that all the Curators should become joint labourers in drawing up a descriptive catalogue, when Sir Everard Home declared, they say, that it was his special duty, and that he would admit of no participation in its performance. Do you know anything of that allegation?

"*A.* Yes, every word or it is perfectly true; I heard him declare it. The trustees had been frequently urging the Board of Curators to make progress in the catalogue, and as they saw that no progress was making in it, they became anxious on the subject. . . . From 1817 to 1823, I had no access to any of the manuscripts, except such as he brought with him to compare with specimens in the collection, for his own special purposes.

"*Q.* What do you mean by his own special purposes?

AFTER HUNTER

"*A.* When he was preparing for his lectures, or drawing up papers for the Philosophical Transactions.

"*Q.* When was it that you first received any information as to the destruction of the manuscripts?

"*A.* In July, 1823, I first obtained a knowledge of the circumstance from Sir Everard himself. He began by telling me that on that very week his house had nearly been on fire; that the engines came, and the firemen insisted upon entrance, as they saw the flames coming out of the chimney. Then he told me that it was in burning the manuscripts of Mr. Hunter that the fire occurred. This conversation passed in a chaise on our road to Kew, where there was a monthly meeting called the 'medico-botanical.' I can hardly describe my feelings on receiving this information. I said to him, 'I hope, Sir Everard, you have not destroyed those ten volumes relating to the gallery, and Mr. Hunter's lectures.' He replied that he had; and then I mentioned to him perhaps twenty others, of which I had a very perfect recollection (and I felt that all the hopes which I had entertained were entirely frustrated and destroyed; my life had been spent in the service of that collection, and I hoped to have lived to see those papers beneficially employed); but he told me that they were all gone, and then I said to him, 'Well, Sir Everard, there is only one thing more to do, and that is to burn the collection itself.' That week Sir Everard had received back from the printer the last proof of his second volume of 'Lectures on Comparative Anatomy'; and I knew that he had used these papers very largely in the preparation of that work."

When Mr. Clift gave his evidence, eleven years after the destruction of the manuscripts, he broke down and cried. Sir Everard, of course, defended himself. He said that Hunter, when he was dying, told him to destroy the manuscripts.[1] He said they were in such a state that they were unfit for publication; but Hunter had so prized them that three of the folios were put at his side when Reynolds painted him. Finally, he said he had destroyed every one of the manuscripts; yet when the trustees brought pressure to bear upon him, he returned several. He faced the matter out, kept his seat on the Council, wrote to the Secretary of the College :—

SACKVILLE STREET, *March* 9, 1824.

SIR,—I beg you will acquaint the Board of Curators, that Mr. Hunter desired that, after his death, his manuscripts should not be entrusted to anybody, but were to be destroyed, being in too imperfect a state for the public eye.

With a view to afford every material that could assist in the formation of the Catalogue, I spent my

---

[1] See Mr. Clift's evidence, Q. 230. But probably Sir Everard did not say that Hunter, when he was dying, told him to destroy the manuscripts; but said that Hunter told him to destroy the manuscripts when he was dead. Even this statement is hard to believe.

leisure hours in the Museum for ten years, taking every assistance these papers could afford, and at the end of thirty years (1793–1823), my own health becoming precarious, I closed my executorship by destroying them.

I am, Sir, yours truly,

EVERARD HOME.

Mr. Belfour, Secretary, Royal College of Surgeons.

He was nearing old age—sixty-seven—when he burned the manuscripts; had been Master and President of the College, twice Hunterian Orator, fifteen years Serjeant-Surgeon to the King, ten years a Baronet. He had been appointed Surgeon to St. George's Hospital when Hunter died, had taken Hunter's lectures, and was Mrs. Hunter's brother; he stood in the dead man's shoes, a great man himself, always under the shadow of the dead man's memory; it is not strange that as he came toward the threescore years and ten he got weary of the sight of the manuscripts, and persuaded himself that they might be burned, now that Hunter had been dead for thirty years. Unhappily for his good name, he had made use of them in his own writings. "As he grew old, he became, I believe, the subject of one of those forms of senile degeneration in morality against which all men growing old need to guard. He stole from the Hunterian manuscripts, and then burnt them, after publishing many of Hunter's observations as his own." And Sir Benjamin Brodie, praising him in the Hunterian Oration for 1837, yet admitted that "unfortunately for his reputation, his ambition rather increased than diminished, while his mental powers were gradually declining. In his latter days, he had an overweening anxiety to appear before the world as a discoverer; and many of his later communications to the Royal Society are of such a nature that his friends must now regret that they were ever published."

The manuscripts that he destroyed are enumerated in Mr. Clift's evidence; nine folio volumes of notes on the dissections of animals, and one on the natural history of vegetables; the lectures on surgery; notes for the Croonian lectures; the natural history of fossils, observations on surgery, cases, and a very large quantity of notes on comparative anatomy, physiology, and experiments. Two of the folios, supposed to be burnt, were afterward recovered.

The loss was remedied by the transcripts made by Mr. Clift. He had copied all the nine folios; the folio on vegetables had not been burned, nor had the notes on fossils, and on the development of the chick. He had moreover copied twenty-six other monographs. The lectures on surgery were saved, for Hunter's pupils had taken shorthand notes of them. The observations on surgery, and on scrofula and cancer, and some of the cases, were lost. In 1861, Sir Richard Owen edited Mr. Clift's copies, and such other monographs

AFTER HUNTER

as had been saved, in two volumes, under the title "Essays and Observations on Natural History, Anatomy, Physiology, Psychology, and Geology, by John Hunter."

Dr. Matthew Baillie died on September 23, 1823, a few weeks after the burning of the manuscripts. Sir Everard Home died in 1832. Mr. Clift died in 1849, having devoted himself for more than half a century to the cause of Hunter's work. His son, Mr. Home Clift, and his son-in-law, Sir Richard Owen, assisted him; and after him came men having the spirit of Hunter, who are still among us; one, above all others, the true heir of all that he left. I have tried to put in a straightforward way the facts of Hunter's life, illustrating them from his own writings, and from the letters and reminiscences of those who were nearest to him. His praise is in every Hunterian Oration, from men most famous in his profession; I have only put together such notes about him as may show to all readers something of his character, something of his work.

I.

London, *August* 31, 1804.

My dear Mrs. Baillie,—I rejoice that I had not heard any of your misfortunes till I heard from yourself this day; here is weather to make you forget them all, and to render even your Rocky coast, and stormy Waves chearful. . . . Poor Baillie, he must pay the price of his celebrity ; if he will be eminent, he must take the consequences ; and who will pity him, I wonder ? I am in hopes, however, he will soon be quite well, and injoy his short excursion, and the sea breezes. We have been gay this week, with all these jaunts, and on Wednesday evg. were at the Play : we had a very good bargain of laughing for our five shillings, and so we ought, for it was extremely warm : . . . So that you see we have still some shreds and patches remaining of the Beau Monde in London. The idea of Invasion is not very strong here, yet we do think of it occasionally, and wish his Majesty would not make such wide sailing excursions from Weymouth ; it would be rather awkward if he were to be caught, and carried over to the Enemy. We are thinking of Preferment and Military Rank in this House from Morning to Night. . . . We have no immediate prospect of John's leaving us,[1] and have some thoughts of making a Party, when Lady Susan leaves us next week, to visit the General and his Lady for a few days . . . All our loves attend you, Baillie, and the Children, compts. to your Brother, and present our kind remembrances to your Neighbour the Ocean,

---

[1] This is her son, who was in the Army. The next letter shows that he became estranged from her : I have omitted part of it on that account. We know very little about him : I believe he was married, for notice was sent to Mr. Clift, in 1830, of the death of Mrs. Hunter, of Gateshead. His mother died in 1821.

for whom we have a very unfeigned regard. Adieu, my Dear Mrs. Baillie, and Believe me Ever with sincere Attachment very Affectionately yours

Anne Hunter.

II.

When Mrs. Hunter died, her property was sworn at under £6,000. Eleven years before her death, she wrote to Dr. Matthew Baillie about her affairs. The letter is dated December 9, 1810, Lower Grosvenor Street :—

My dear Baillie,—As at any Age it is but prudent to settle ones Worldly Affairs, at mine it is peculiarly proper. Before I became acquainted with the situation of my poor unhappy Son, I had conceived that leaving behind me a mere Memoir of my Wishes, to be fulfilled after my Death by my Children, would be sufficient: but circumstances are now changed, and I am obliged to think differantly. As in case of my Death, I believe Agnes would not immediately be capable of acting, I have one favour to ask of your Friendship, in addition to many already received, which is, that you will join your name with my Brother, as my Executors. My funded property is, as you know, small. . . . I have drawn out a sketch of my Will, which I daresay is very awkwardly done, but you shall see it, and give me your opinion. I have, in fact, so little to leave, that it is principaly made up of little remembrances to friends, which were the articles in my former Paper of Memoirs, and which I have now only put in a new form, that I might make one principle alteration. I have not made the proposition yet to my Brother, but I think *he* cannot well refuse me this last act of complaisance. Adieu, my Dear Friend, I am to the last moment of my life, Affectionately Yours

A. Hunter.

APPENDIX

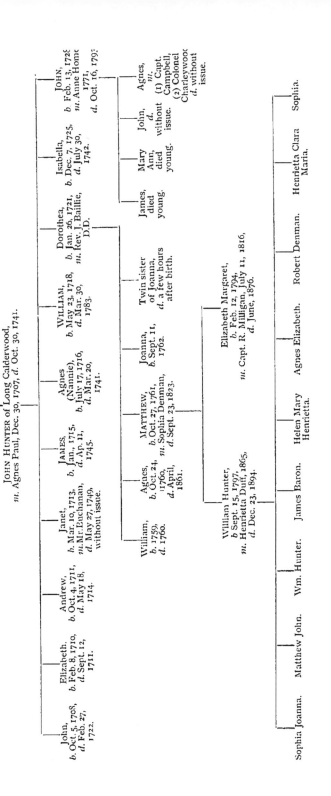

CHIEF REFERENCES

1. "The Works of John Hunter, F.R.S.: with Notes." Edited by James F. Palmer. In four volumes. London, Longmans, 1835. With a Life, by Drewry Ottley.
2. "Treatise on the Blood, Inflammation, and Gunshot Wounds." By John Hunter. With a Life, by Sir Everard Home. Edited in 1794.
3. "Essays and Observations on Natural History, Anatomy, Physiology, Psychology, and Geology." By John Hunter, F.R.S. Being his posthumous papers on those subjects. In two volumes. Edited by Richard Owen, F.R.S., D.C.L. London, Longmans, 1861.
4. The Baillie Letters. Presented by Miss Baillie to the Royal College of Surgeons. Also letters, &c., from Miss Baillie's private collection.
5. Mr. J. B. Bailey's Collection, at the Royal College of Surgeons, of pictures, newspaper cuttings, &c., relating to Hunter.
6. "Memoirs of the Life and Doctrines of the late John Hunter, Esq." By Joseph Adams, M.D. London, 1817.
7. "The Life of John Hunter." By Jesse Foot, Surgeon. London, 1794.

APPENDIX

8. "Two Great Scotsmen (William and John Hunter)." By George Mather, M.D.
9. "William Smellie and his Contemporaries." By John Glaister, M.D. Glasgow, 1894.
10. Pettigrew's "Medical Portrait Gallery." 1838.
11. "Dictionary of National Biography."
12. "Lives of British Physicians." London, John Murray, 1830.
13. "Life of Edward Jenner." By John Baron, M.D. Two volumes. London, 1838.
14. "Leicester Square." By Tom Taylor.
15. "An Account of the Life and Writings of the late William Hunter, M.D., F.R.S." By Samuel Foart Simmons, M.D., F.R.S. London, 1783.
16. "John Hunter at Earl's Court, Kensington." By S. S. M. (Dr. Merriman). 1881.
17. "Introductory Address at St. George's Hospital on the Centenary of John Hunter's Death." By Timothy Holmes, F.R.C.S., Consulting Surgeon to the Hospital. London, Adlard & Sons, 1893.
18. "Autobiography of the late Sir Benjamin Brodie, Bart." Edited by his son. London, Longmans, 1865.
19. "St. George's Hospital: Some Account of the Hospital and School." By William Emmanuel Page, M.D. London, 1866. (From the first volume of the St. George's Hospital Reports.)
20. *The Lancet*, July 11, 1835. (Mr. Clift's evidence before the Parliamentary Medical Committee.)
21. The Hunterian Orations, from 1814 onwards.
22. "Physiological Lectures." By John Abernethy, F.R.S. London, Longmans, 1817.
23. *British Medical Journal.* Medical Institutions.

APPENDIX

24. "Catalogue of the Hunterian Relics exhibited at the Royal College of Surgeons of England on Wednesday, July 5, 1893." By J. B. Bailey.
25. "Only an Old Chair." By D. R. A. G. M. (Dr. Goodsir). Edinburgh, 1884.
26. "Catalogue of the Portraits at the Royal College of Surgeons." By E. Hallett.
27. *The Lancet*, May 9, 1896. Dr. Newton Pitt's Oration.
28. "Hunter and his Pupils." S. D. Gross, 1881.
29. *British Medical Journal*, 1890, i. 738, 865. Dr. Finlayson's Account of Mr. Clift.
30. Hunterian Society's Transactions, 1896–97. The Annual Oration. By Dr. Hingston Fox.

INDEX

A

Abernethy, 104, 121, 221, 226, 230
Adair, 52, 73, 115, 184
Adams, 153, 218, 221, 238
Albinus, 25
Alloa, 65
Antoinette, Marie, 219
Armstrong, 41
Auckland, 240

B

Baillie, Agnes, 22, 23
Baillie, James, 22, 74, 119
Baillie, Joanna, 22, 27, 119, 192
BAILLIE, MATTHEW: birth, 22; education, 237; with Wm. Hunter, 65, 237; gives Long Calderwood to John Hunter, 237; his executor, 236; death, 257; letters from Mrs. Hunter, 257–260
Baillie, William Hunter, 26
Baillie, Miss, 27, 190, 239
Banks, Sir J., 145, 242
St. Bartholomew's Hospital, 48, 213, 214
Bath, 114, 135, 145, 169
Bayford, 92
Bell, William, 112, 183
Belleisle, 53, 72–77
Berkeley, Lord, 121
Black, Mrs., 130
Blane, Sir Gilbert, 174
Blizard, Sir William, 221
Blyth, Dr., 77
Boughton, Sir Theodosius, 229
Bristol, 135
Brooks, 86, 177
Buckland, Frank, 88, 235
Buller, Mr. Justice, 229
Byron, Lady, 193

C

Campbell, Sir James, 191
Carlisle, Sir Anthony, 224
Carter, Mrs. E., 191

INDEX

Castle Lane, 194
Castle Street, 154, 159, 182, 244
Cattgal, 137
Chappell Street, 194
Charleywood, Col., 192
Cheselden, 48, 195
Cheston, 144
Clarke, Dr., 222
Clench, 170
CLIFT, WILLIAM : birth and boyhood, 243 ; work with Hunter, 244 ; Conservator of Museum, 246 ; transcribes Hunter's manuscripts, 244, 256 ; evidence before Committee, 250–254 ; death, 247
Cline, 104
Cogan, Dr., 56
College of Surgeons, 229, 243–245
Combe, Dr., 71
Cooper, Sir Astley, 105, 121
Covent Garden, 23, 34, 41, 60
Cruikshank, 118, 225
Cullen, 23, 29, 40, 45, 65, 81

D

D'Arblay, Mme., 191
Darwin, 19, 51

Donellan, Captain, 229, 233
Douglas, James, 24, 28, 38
Douglas, John, 23, 33, 37, 41
Douglas, Miss, 24, 34, 41
Douglas, Mrs., 33, 38, 41

E

Earl's Court, 85–91, 111, 120, 239
Edgeworth, Miss, 192

F

Farquarson, 115
Finlayson, Dr., 154
Foot, Jesse, 32, 85, &c.
Fordyce, 69, 123, 134, 174, 187
France, 38, 42

G

Gainsborough, 65
Garrow, Dr., 58
Garthshore, Dr., 98
Gataker, 92
St. George's Hospital, 49, 50, 194–219
Giant, the Irish, 89, 155
Gilbert, Mrs., 243
Glasgow, 27, 36
Glasgow College, 23, 237
Golden Square, 53, *sqq.*
Gross, Prof., 121
Grosvenor, Lord, 196
Gunning, 198, 202, *sqq.*

INDEX

Guy, 93
Guy's Hospital, 214

H

Haller, 59
Hamilton, Francis, 28
Hawkins, Cæsar, 198; Charles, 199; George, 199
Haydn, 97
Haymarket, the, 102
Haynes, 250
Hazeland, 171
Heberden, 122
Hewson, 84, 141
Hicks, 132, 139
Hodgson, Genl., 53, 75
Hogarth, 157
Holmes, Mr. T., 240
Home, Miss (Mrs. Hunter's sister), 191, 192
Home, Robert, 45
Home, Robert Boyne, 95
HOME, SIR EVERARD: his account of himself, 99; goes to Plymouth, 115; comes back, 161; at Leicester Square, 170; assistant surgeon at St. George's, 200; surgeon, 255; takes Hunter's lectures, 186; his executor, 236; the story of the manuscripts, 250–255; death, 256

Howison, 89
Hume, David, 81
HUNTER, JOHN: his father, 20, 25; his mother, 20, 25, 33; brothers and sisters, 20–45; birth and boyhood, 20–32, 35; at Glasgow, 27, 36; early years in London, 46, 52; Oxford, 27, 50; Belleisle and Portugal, 52-55, 72–80; Golden Square and Earl's Court, 83–91; F.R.S., 91; Surgeon to St. George's Hospital, 92; marriage, 93; lectures, 102; Jerymn Street, 95; Surgeon to the King, 113; Croonian lectures. 113; work on the teeth, 93, 115; death of William Hunter, 117; letters to James Baillie, 119, to Jenner, 121, *sqq.*; illnesses, 52, 101, 150–172, 184, *sqq.*; operation for aneurysm, 171; works on venereal disease and on animal œconomy, 173, 183; Deputy-Surgeon-General, 174; work on whales, 177, on bees, 186, 249, on the blood, inflammation, and gunshot

INDEX

HUNTER, JOHN (*continued*)—
wounds, 53 ; Copley medal, 179 ; portraits by Home, 45, Reynolds, 179; Surgeon-General, 184; St. George's Hospital, 49, 50, 194, *sqq.* ; death, 219 ; Westminster Abbey, 235; sale of his property, 236, 239 ; his museum, 243–249

HUNTER, WILLIAM : birth and boyhood, 22, 29 ; early life in London, 24, *sqq.* ; letters to his mother, 37, to James, 39, 42 ; appointments, 45, 65 ; school of anatomy, 46 ; Medical Commentaries, 56, *sqq.* ; museum and art collection, 65 ; Great Windmill Street, 66 ; Atlas, 67 ; quarrel with John Hunter, 67–70 ; death, 71

HUNTER, MRS, 95–99, 120, 158, 221, 232, 235 ; reminiscences of her grandniece, 190 ; letters, 169, 192, 257–260

Hunter, Agnes (J. H.'s sister), 20, 43

Hunter, Agnes (J. H.'s daughter), 97, 191, 192

Hunter, Andrew, 20
Hunter, Dorothea (Mrs. Baillie), 22, 49, 64, 237
Hunter, Elizabeth, 20
Hunter, Francis, 20, 28
Hunter, Isabella (Tibbie), 20, 38
Hunter, James (J. H.'s brother), 21, 29, 39, 42
Hunter, James (J. H.'s son), 96, 119
Hunter, John (J. H.'s father), 20, 25
Hunter, John (J. H.'s son), 8, 158, 236, 258
Hunter, John (J. H.'s brother), 20
Hunter, Janet (Mrs. Buchanan), 21, 35
Hunter, Mary Ann (J. H.'s daughter), 96, 119
Hunter, Mrs. (J. H.'s mother), 20, 25, 33
Hunter of Hunterston, 19, 33

I

Ingham, 78

J

Jenner, Edward, 121–146, 163–186
Jenner, Henry, 158
Jermyn Street, 46, 95, *sqq.*
Johnson, Dr., 65

INDEX

K
Keate, 200–202, 217
Keppel, Commodore, 115
Kingston, John, 93

L
Lanesborough House, 195
Lawrence, Sir William, 230
Leicester Square, 154–160, 182, 239
Lions' Den, The, 87, 239
London Hospital, 214, 215
Long Calderwood, 20, *sqq.*, 49, 237
Loudoun, Lord, 78
Luders, 138
Lyceum Medicum, 183, 188
Lynn, William, 228

M
Macaulay, Dr., 74, 75
Mackenzie, Col., 75
Mackenzie, Dr., 68
Madox, 78
Manningham, Sir Richard, 46
Marshall, Dr., 174
Martin's-in-the-Fields, St., 97, 235
Mather, Dr., 66
Mead, Dr., 195
Merriman, Dr., 87
Middleton, 174
Milligan, Mrs., 190

Monro, Alex., sen., 23, 40
Monro, Alex., jun., 57, 58, 62, 77
Monro, Donald, 59
Montagu, Mrs., 192

N
Nicholls, Frank, 24
Nicol, George, 173, 222, 225

O
Orford, Lord, 191
Ottley, 46, 87, 111, 122, &c.
Oxford, 27, 49, 237
Owen, Dr., 41
Owen, Sir Richard, 161, 248, 256

P
Paris, 25, 34, 42
Pettigrew, 75, 77
Physick, 121, 233
Plunkett, 109
Pine, 44
Pitcairn, 74, 76, 108, 168, 174
Pitt, William, 240
Pitt, Dr. Newton, 187
Portugal, 53, 76
Pott, 48, 60, 181
Power, Mr. D'Arcy, 49

INDEX

Q
Queensberry, Duke of, 224
Queen Street, 215

R
Reynolds, Sir Joshua, 44, 179, 229
Robertson, Dr., 219
Rumsey, Nathaniel, 110

S
Sandys, Dr., 46
Sennertus, 109
Sharp, W., 157, 179, 180
Sharpe, S., 24
Sloane, Sir Hans, 195
Smellie, Dr., 23, 34, 41, 46
Smollett, 29, 76
Societies, Medical, 183, 187
Stevenson, R. L., 155
Stewart, Prof., 248
St. Thomas' Hospital, 195, 214
Swift, 231

T
Taylor of Whitworth, 168
Thomas, Sir N., 108
Thomas, 223
Thomson, 121
Thurlow, Bishop, 168
Townsend, 79
Tunbridge, 169
Tyrawly, Lord, 78
Tyrwhitt, 79

V
Vesalius, 66, 233

W
Walker, William, 199, 202
Warren, Dr., 108
Westminster Abbey, 235
Westminster Hospital, 195
Westminster Infirmary, 194
Wilkins, 196
Windmill Street, 66, 215
Woollett, 110, 157

Y
Young, Prof., 66
Young, 77–79

Z
Zoffany, 44, 157
Zuccarelli, 157

Printed in Great Britain
by Amazon.co.uk, Ltd.,
Marston Gate.